KOREAN BUSINESSES

STUDIES IN ASIA PACIFIC BUSINESS
ISSN 1369-7153

General Editors: Robert Fitzgerald, Chris Rowley and Paul Stewart

Greater China: Political Economy, Inward Investment and Business Culture
Edited by Chris Rowley and Mark Lewis

Beyond Japanese Management: The End of Modern Times?
Edited by Paul Stewart

Management in China: The Experiences of Foreign Businesses
Edited by Roger Strange

**Human Resource Management in the Asia Pacific Region:
Convergence Questioned**
Edited by Chris Rowley

**Korean Businesses:
Internal and External Industrialization**
Edited by Chris Rowley and Johngseok Bae

KOREAN BUSINESSES:
Internal and External Industrialization

Edited by

CHRIS ROWLEY
City University Business School, London

and

JOHNGSEOK BAE
Hanyang University, Seoul

FRANK CASS
LONDON • PORTLAND, OR

First published in 1998 in Great Britain by
FRANK CASS AND COMPANY LIMITED
Newbury House, 900 Eastern Avenue, London IG2 7HH, England

and in the United States of America by
FRANK CASS
c/o ISBS, Inc.
5804 N.E. Hassalo Street, Portland, Oregon 97213-3644

Transferred to Digital Printing 2004

Website: http://www.frankcass.com

Copyright © 1998 Frank Cass & Co. Ltd.

British Library Cataloguing in Publication Data

Korean businesses : internal and external
industrialization. – (Studies in Asia Pacific business)
1. Business enterprises – Korea 2. Korea – Economic
conditions
I. Rowley, Chris, 1959- II. Bae, Johngseok
330.9'519

ISBN 0 7146 4483 8

ISBN 0 7146 4924 4 (hbk)
ISBN 0 7146 4483 8 (pbk)
ISSN 1369-7153

Library of Congress Cataloging-in-Publication Data

Korean businesses : internal and external industrialization / edited by
Chris Rowley and Johngseok Bae.
  p. cm. – (Studies in Asia Pacific business, ISSN 1369-7153)
  "This group of studies first appeared in a special issue of Asia
Pacific business review, vol. 4, nos 2&3, winter 1997/spring 1998"-
-verso t.p.
  Includes index.
  ISBN 0-7146-4924-4. – ISBN 0-7146-4483-8 (pbk.)
  1. Industrialization–Korea (South) 2. Korea (South)–Economic
conditions–20th century. 3. Electronic industries–Korea (South)
4. Corporations, Korean. 5. Industrial management–Korea (South)
I. Rowley, Chris, 1956-   . II. Bae, Johngseok. III. Series.
HC467.K619864 1998
338.95195–dc21   98-26372
                                                          CIP

This group of studies first appeared in a Special Issue of *Asia Pacific Business Review* (ISSN
1360-2381), Vol. 4, Nos 2&3 (Winter 1997/Spring 1998) [Korean Business: Internal and
External Industrialization].

DEDICATION

To the memory of Anne Rowley, 1907–1997:
A wonderful matriarch missed by many

Contents

Introduction: The Icarus Paradox in Korean Business and Management

CHRIS ROWLEY and JOHNGSEOK BAE

For some time, many have viewed newly industrializing economies (NIEs), especially the 'Asian Tigers', as a major force that will lead world economic growth in the coming era, with much talk of a 'Pacific Century' and economies poised to leap ahead of those of the US and Europe. Much in Asia has inspired pride at home and envy abroad. Such expectations have diminished in the wake of the recent financial crisis in many Asian countries (see Cathie[1] in this volume). Thus, plunging currencies and stockmarkets, and swelling foreign debt burdens in local currencies 'have put the economic miracle in deep freeze' (*The Economist*, 1998: 3). Numerous news items are somewhat cynically headlined 'from miracle to crisis' or 'from tiger to beggar'. Self-confidence has evaporated with stories of people handing over gold jewellery to boost foreign reserves! However, it is useful to remember that there is no one 'Asian model'; the economies hugely differ in structure and political systems and policies pursued (*The Economist*, ibid.; Cathie).

Some writers argue that modern history reveals 'cycles' in economic leadership among countries (Kennedy, 1987; Kogut, 1993). Lazonick (1991) contends that the first three leaders possessed different types of capitalism: Britain was associated with 'proprietary capitalism', Germany and the US with 'managerial capitalism', and Japan with 'collective capitalism'. Britain, Germany and the US, as 'forerunners' in the process of industrialization, used inventions and innovations as major sources of capability creation (see van Hoesel). On the other hand, NIEs, following different routes of industrialization, have been called 'latecomers' (*vis-à-vis* the first group[2]). Latecomers relied more on imitating, borrowing or learning advanced technological and organizational capabilities to achieve their national industrialization and eventually to gain 'national competitiveness' (now a trendy, though nebulous, concept[3]). Such growth is seen to stem from several sources.

This volume is focused on the Korean[4] model of industrialization and economic growth, internationalization, organizational capabilities and management, and inherent disadvantages. The subject matter covered includes the sources of growth and industrialization, the 'catch-up' strategies of firms, foreign investment, and the causes of the recent financial crisis and future possibilities. This introductory piece has been written to

Chris Rowley, City University Business School, London; Johngseok Bae, Hanyang University, Korea.

provide a contextual introduction to the topic with four main sections. A brief summary of the driving forces underpinning Korean industrialization and economic growth is followed by the perspectives and main contents of the volume. For reasons of topicality, the next section deals with the recent financial crisis, and links are made to longer term trends. Finally, some concluding points are made.

'DRIVING FORCES' FOR INDUSTRIALIZATION AND ECONOMIC GROWTH

Previous studies have shown quite diverse perspectives on the principal engine of industrialization in Korea. Some credited its economic success to government (Amsden, 1989), and others to management and the private sector (Westphal, 1982; Kim, 1997a), or even 'well educated' people (Moore and Jennings, 1995). Chung *et al.* (1997) produce a long and disparate list of influencing 'conditions' they call 'design' (or internal: economic growth policies, administrative structure, large business groups, public enterprise, productive skill development, managerial practice) and 'contextual' (or external: commitment to work, high achievement needs, new Confucian culture, development minded elite, absence of retrogressive groups, international business elite). For them, while contextual factors provided the economy with opportunities, design factors were manipulated by policymakers to produce desired outcomes. However, viewpoints seem to be a matter of emphasis.

'State' versus 'Free Market' Views

There is a continuing macro-level debate between the government intervention perspective and the free market view (Amsden, 1989; World Bank, 1993). The former stresses the critical role of the state as a driving force of economic development and growth, while the latter ascribes it to the free market (see Cathie). Interestingly, Rodrick (1998), by using an 'index' of 'institutional quality', and adjusting it for income per head and education, shows nearly all differences in Asian growth can be explained by the 'quality' of an economy's institutions. Governments in the NIEs played several critical roles, such as significant employers, regulators, and conscious policymakers of a system that enveloped the mutual inter-relations of workers, management and government (Dunlop, 1958). As the 'prime agent' of industrialization, government stimulated the economy by providing incentives, such as long term loans with low interest rates. If we borrow Thompson's (1967) organization theory, Korean governments tried to adapt environments (for example, foreign investment) by reducing risks, though Korea has a remarkably low proportion of direct foreign investment; instead, joint ventures and licensing have been used as vehicles for technology transfer. The technical level, however, was 'sealed-off' to pursue efficiency. In this sense, governments provided Korean firms with nurturing environments to facilitate the formation of large, diversified business conglomerates, the *chaebols*. From the 1960s, government raised capital for a select group of successful and 'loyal' entrepreneurs and nurtured them with low interest rates, preferential taxes, import-export licences and acquisitions of governmental properties at below market prices (Chung *et al.*, 1997). In the 1970s such groups were called upon to launch new ventures in targeted sectors and again provided with various subsidies and incentives. The result was high growth and diversification: between 1973 and 1978, some 46 large *chaebols* grew at an average annual rate of almost 23 per cent (ibid.). Thus, 'The government was the planner and businesses were the implementer' [*sic*] (ibid.: 11), as the state used selected enterprises as its instrument for economic development.

Thus, we can give credit to government for the earlier stages of Korean economic development. One feature of government is therefore worth emphasizing. The success of the NIEs was realized by the 'visible hand' of strong authoritarian government rather than by the 'invisible hand' of the free market. This is a story of 'government success'. The first stage of Korean industrialization can be characterized as political economy (government led economic development) on the assumption that the market was immature.

'Internal' versus 'External' Factors

The macro state versus free market debate is mainly focused on growth generated by internal, rather than external,[5] factors. In contrast, Castley's key argument is that the main driving force for the growth of the Korean electronics industry stemmed from external sources (see also Castley, 1997). He argues that growth came from neither the government nor local entrepreneurs, but foreign interests (especially the restructuring Japanese electronics industry), and was not so much a national as a regional phenomenon. Japanese firms played a critical role by investing in Korea during the early period of industrialization, and even until the 1980s. As Castley explains, Japanese firms took advantage of geographical proximity and had self-interested motives: searching for lower wages; upgrading their domestic production facilities; and achieving 'triangular trade patterns'.[6]

On the other hand, Korean governments and corporate management also took advantage of these conditions. Through the growth and learning periods, Korean industries became global players. Indeed, whatever the 'donor' countries' motives, host economies built up their own capabilities. For example, as Kim (1997b) explains, when Samsung had difficulties in transferring technology, it relied on several different strategic avenues: seeking alternative sources of technology; buying it from financially troubled, small American firms; developing its own technology; or entering a consortium with other local competitors to develop technology. The improvement in capabilities then became a threat to the original donor countries themselves (however, it is not clear that other countries, for example in sub-Saharan Africa, have also always been able to do so).

As Ernst and O'Connor (1992) and Castley observe, we now find a similar 'dependence' of South East Asian countries (such as Thailand, Malaysia, the Philippines) on Japan and the NIEs, just as we saw the dependence of the Korean electronics industry on the Japanese. Likewise, Kim points out that Korean firms moved into China with similar motives to those of Japanese firms in Korea. Now China has started to penetrate international markets with its lower prices. It could be argued that such a development exemplifies the flow of technology, displaying the idea of an 'industrial life cycle' migration around the world (Vernon, 1966), though this has been modified (Vernon, 1979; Utterback, 1994) and criticized, for instance for its universalism, determinism and levels of analysis (Rowley, 1998a). Various types of manufacture, and aspects within production, are seen to become more or less important to countries over time. Hobday adds a new dimension to classical theories concerning the location of production: the role of domestic firms. Building local firms' capabilities is a necessary condition for such relocation. There is a flow of some technology in world industries. The transfer occurred originally from the 'firstcomers' to 'followers' (such as Japan), then from followers to latecomers, and now from latecomers to 'late-latecomers' (such as China, Thailand). As Kim (1997b: 97) notes, 'it is difficult for foreign firms to restrict the outflow of technology'.

In sum, Castley raises a perceptive point that has been understressed. What is less obvious are the conditions under which factor disadvantages can be converted into competitive advantage and through catch-up strategies at the firm level (see Porter, 1990). So, we now need to look into more micro-level activities.

'Macro' versus 'Micro' approaches

When we assume that national competitiveness (but see note 3 again) comes from core industries' capabilities and eventually from individual firm's capabilities, then we need to look into firm-level activities. Without fine tuned firm-level analysis we are unable to obtain a full explanation (Kim, 1997a). Hobday illuminates this aspect clearly. This line of argument is also related to the 'factor accumulation' versus 'technological progress' debate. The World Bank (1993) identified three key factors in East Asia's economic success: inexpensive labour with a strong work ethic, high saving rates, and increased labour productivity through technological innovation. However, Krugman (1994b) perceptively argued that there had not really been a 'miracle'; rather, Asian innovation and productivity had been overestimated. Rapid growth was simply the result of heavy investment and large increases in employment. Therefore, it was the result of 'perspiration, not inspiration', and not sustainable – once spare labour was used up and capital per worker reaches rich country standards you will get diminishing returns and growth will slow (ibid.). More may well agree with this now than before the Asian crisis.

We can explain Korean industrialization and economic growth by showing how firms have built their capabilities. As Porter (1990) argued, each country takes different routes to its competitiveness (for an illuminating application of Porterian analysis to Asia see Fitzgerald, 1994 and the contributors therein). A nation's competitiveness, according to Porter, comes from the capabilities of its industry in innovating and upgrading. As a latecomer, what were Korean firms' strategies for gaining and sustaining competitive advantages? How could Korean firms shift from imitator to innovator, from original equipment manufacturer (OEM) producer to global player, and from exporter to direct investor?

As some writers have noted (Amsden, 1989; Kim, 1997a), the conceptualization of the industrialization process in Korea as a 'learning process' is an excellent point. Recent literature on organizational learning has emphasized knowledge creation, transference, and institutionalization (see, *inter alia*, Senge, 1990; Garvin, 1993; Nonaka, 1994). As Kim (1997a) suggests, for firms in latecomer nations, there are several sources of technical learning and all are affected by factors, as listed in Table 1.

TABLE 1
SOURCES AND FACTORS IN TECHNOLOGICAL LEARNING

Sources	Affecting Factors
* international community	* market and technological environment
* domestic community (firm's environment)	* public policy
* in-house efforts at firm level (firm's activities)	* formal education
	* organizational structure

Source: From Kim (1997a).

To catch up in organizational and technological capabilities, 'crisis construction' and 'crisis management' have been popularly used, among others, in the automobile and semiconductor industries; and visionary entrepreneurs used crisis construction as a strategic means of opportunistic and discontinuous learning (ibid.). With such approaches, firms deliberately impose a series of crisis ('a sense of crisis') on employees by demanding them to achieve overly ambitious goals within a certain time period to create environments in which discontinuous learning could then taken place. For dynamic learning processes at the firm level, 'absorptive capacity' is critical (see Cohen and Levinthal, 1990). This is 'the ability to exploit external knowledge' or 'the ability of a firm to recognize the value of new, external information, assimilate it, and apply it to commercial ends' (ibid.: 128). Two important elements in technological learning are the existing knowledge base, and the intensity of effort (Kim, 1997a). For tomorrow's increased knowledge, it is necessary to have today's knowledge. However, without the second element (commitment or conscious effort), it is difficult for learning to take place. Samsung used crisis creation and management to catch up in the semiconductor industry during its attempt to leapfrog from being a mere simple device assembler to emerge as a world leader in memory chip parts (Kim, 1997b).

Management alone, therefore, was not sufficient for creating, transferring and institutionalizing knowledge in order to obtain competitiveness. As Porter (1990) explained in his now famous 'diamond' structure, four factors determine national competitive advantage: firm strategy, structure and rivalry; factor conditions; related and supporting industries; and demand conditions (for some development of this and a Korean application, see Cho, 1994). Therefore, other necessary conditions are required for successful learning along with management initiative. These include government supports, well educated human resources, suppliers and organizational linkages and relationships (see, *inter alia*, Piore and Sabel, 1984; Rowley, 1994, 1996[7]). However, although all these factors contributed to successful learning, one obvious point is that it was not possible without the capabilities and catch-up strategies of latecomer firms (see Hobday).

PERSPECTIVES AND CONTENTS

As we have seen, Castley focuses on the external sources of industrialization and concentrates on a restricted time period (1967–76). He stresses the significance of the international environment. Thus, foreign countries and firms played critical roles in Korean industrialization by providing relevant technology, capital and markets. He also points out the dependence of Korean firms on Japanese firms because of a lack of technology and suppliers, a situation that continued even until the late 1980s. However, this macro-level analysis does not adequately emphasize the firm-level process of building technological capabilities.

To supplement such perspectives we can look at Hobday. This illustrates how Samsung Electronics Company (SEC) of Korea and ACER of Taiwan overcame both technological and market disadvantages (for other Korea–Taiwan comparisons, see Koo, 1987; Lau, 1990; McDermott, 1992; other useful comparisons include Redding, 1990; Appelbaum and Henderson, 1992; Whitley, 1992). Hobday argues that SEC and ACER made technological and market transitions through imitation and catch-up strategies, moving from OEM to original design and manufacture and then to original brand manufacture. By providing a model of a latecomer firm's progress, Hobday neatly and succinctly captures the paths and mechanisms of learning in these firms. In doing so, he juxtaposes SEC and ACER to contrast the different features of each firm.

Similarly, Kim uses the SEC case to investigate expansion into international production (into China) and the ways to gain and sustain competitive advantage. By employing several theoretical perspectives, he reveals that SEC could gain competitive advantage through the development of production capability, such as integrated production networks. However, as Kim points out, there are also several weaknesses, namely the centralized interaction between headquarters and foreign subsidiaries in marketing and research and development (R&D) areas, which prevents SEC getting on-the-spot information (contributions to Slater and Strange, 1997, include analysis of the international and control style of Korean companies). Kim concludes that SEC's overseas production capability is temporary because it can be overtaken by indigenous firms; and its lack of organizational and technological capabilities are major liabilities and cannot match established multinational companies (MNCs).

Furthermore, van Hoesel utilizes two Korean (including SEC) and two Taiwanese leading firms in electronics that had invested in Europe to show their prospects and limitations (see also McDermott, 1992; contributions to Slater and Strange, 1997). First, he argues that latecomer Korean and Taiwanese MNCs differ from MNCs of firstcomer countries mainly due to their different industrialization paradigm. Also, other examples of firms from the two economies show different features in terms of investment scale, motivation to invest, global strategy and internationalization patterns. He explains that these variations come from the late industrialization effect, the size of firms in home countries (hence their financial muscle) and firm-specific strategies. However, like the other contributors, he also points out that weaknesses in technological, and especially marketing, capabilities are major obstacles to these firms in building up strong positions in European markets.

The key characteristics of the contributions to this volume (excluding Cathie's contextual macro overview) are summarized in Table 2. Several features are noticeable. First, all the studies deal with the electronics industry, or subsectors of consumer electronics (radios, TVs), industrial electronics (telecommunications) and electronics parts and components (semi-conductors). Why the electronics industry? Partly this is because of its outstanding export performance and rapid growth as electronics took the foremost place in national exports, and its importance to governments and policymakers. For instance, the Korean government, designating electronics a 'strategic export industry', enacted the Electronics Industry Promotion Act (1969) and created the Electronic Industry Promotion Fund (Castley; Kim, 1997a). In 1984 the *chaebols* started to move in to very large scale integrated circuit production. In the case of the semiconductor industry, *chaebols* became major memory chip producers in a mere decade.

Second, the studies cover SEC either directly or indirectly. One reason for this is SEC's exemplary dynamism and innovation. The relatively young SEC showed a rapid growth rate (averaging 60 per cent per year[8]). Its export levels also dramatically increased, from US$ 100 million in 1978 to US$ 10 billion by 1995. SEC leapfrogged from being a mere assembler of simple devices to become one of the world's most innovative producers of dynamic random access memory (DRAM) (see Hobday). It had become independent

TABLE 2
STUDIES INCLUDED BY CHARACTERISTICS

	Castley	Hobday	Kim	Van Hoesel
Relevant Period	1967–1976	Mainly 1975–>	Mainly 1990s	1980s and 1990s
Stage of Development	Start-up period	Entry, catch-up, and leadership stages	Catch-up, and leadership stages	Catch-up, and leadership stages
Industry Covered	Electronics (especially parts and components)	Electronics	Electronics . (especially consumer electronics)	Consumer electronics and (for Taiwanese firms) computer industry
Company Covered	Indirectly: SEC, Hyundai, LGE, Daewoo, etc.	SEC, ACER	SEC	SEC, LGE; ACER, FIC
Main Theme and Focus	Role of Japan in Korean develop- ment; economic dependence	Firm-level catch- up strategies and learning processes; managerial capabilities	SEC in China; its strengths and weaknesses; key value-added	Asian MNCs in Europe; motivations and patterns of internationalization

Key:
SEC = Samsung Electronics
LGE = LG Electronics
FIC = First International Computer

in DRAM design and production in 1988, becoming the leader in 256 megabit DRAM design in 1994, and introducing the one gigabit DRAM in 1996 (Kim, 1997a; Samsung Electronics, 1996). As a result, by 1996 SEC was the largest DRAM producer, with a 17 per cent share of the global market,[9] and the seventh largest semiconductor manufacturer in the world (Samsung Electronics, 1996).

Third, each contribution focuses on different time periods in the history of Korean industrialization. They range from the start-up stage, through the growth phase to the mature period. Furthermore, as a result of the above, the focus and perspective of each study, though complementary, is also quite different from the others. Each author views developments from different angles and emphasizes certain aspects of industrialization, growth, business and management in Korea.

However, there are obvious limitations to these contributors. One is the restricted sectoral focus itself. Another is that they cover developments before the recent Asian financial crisis and Korean problems. What role did the actors discussed above have in this? What impacts will it have on them and the Korean model? We address some of these key questions below.

THE KOREAN MODEL AND RECENT ECONOMIC TROUBLES

Reasons for the Recent Financial Crisis

Cathie argues that the core of the recent Asian financial crisis is attributable to the heart of the 'Asian development model'. Accordingly, the reform of economic policy and industrial restructuring also requires Korea to abandon its model, characterized by utilizing resources for industrialization on a bulky scale with sustained economic growth. Since the formulation of industrial policy, he contends, has neglected the economic and social costs, now Korea is paying the 'price', in high unemployment, social unrest, a drop in consumption and a loss of savings. What is less obvious is possible future policy direction.

The causes of the crisis in Korea (both the dollar liquidity problem and other general economic difficulties) can be broadly placed into two groups: institutional, and (perhaps more fundamentally) social and cultural problems, with each divided into several subcategories (see Table 3). However, institutional problems, including low capital adequacy ratio by international standards,[10] have often been lumped together, somewhat narrowly, as 'structural' problems. Also, the apparent immediate cause for the recent crisis was the sudden reversal of short run capital flows – a speculative crisis. Indeed, the Korean Won fell in value by 50 per cent at the end of 1997, and the stock market by 60 per cent (Cathie).

TABLE 3
UNDERLYING CAUSES OF THE RECENT KOREAN CRISIS

Institutional

- *government related*: lack of coherent economic philosophy, and inconsistency of policies; intimate relationships with banks and businesses; *dirigiste*; financial suppression policies (= easy money and artificially low interest rates)
- *chaebol related*: head-centred governance systems; intersubsidiary loan guarantees; cross investments; exclusive relationships with suppliers with insufficient technical support; excessive and overlapping investments; exorbitant borrowings and reckless expansion
- *finance sector related*: lack of supervisory function over lenders; low capital adequacy ratio by international standards; 'loans' on basis of political connections not cash flow projections and collateral

Sociocultural environment

- *macro*: homogeneous background (language, ethnicity, culture); cultural exclusivism; nationalistic mind set (exclusively functions to prevent foreign direct investment)
- *micro*: regionalism, school relations, and kinship applied to personnel procedures and systems and political arena (political parties based on regions) preventing organizations and society building 'sounder' (based more on 'fairness' and 'honest' factors) systems
- *culture*: of rapid growth (so called *palli palli* or 'quickly, quickly'; *chon-ji* ('gift giving') with symbiotic relations between business–government–political lobbying

While world economic environments have drastically altered, Korean government and management behaviours and practices have shown little change. About a decade ago, a special issue of *World Development* (1988) dealt with the issue of 'industrial restructuring' in Korea as the economy experienced rapid industrial transition. In this, Leipziger (1988: 131) identified financial reform and the business–government compact as agendas for future policy reform, and wisely foretold the tricky tasks Korea should have undertaken by stating that 'financial reform is therefore an urgent matter, best undertaken in a period of buoyant growth'. We should admit that reformist efforts were insufficient to adjust to the changing environment of the world economy.

What then is the role of the state, banking sector and industry in formulating and introducing any potential solutions? According to Zysman (1983), three possible alternative solutions are: state led, market led, and negotiated or intermediate, depending on the characteristics of the financial system. The Korean government played a critical role as a facilitator of industrialization, became an obstacle to further advancement, and is now trying to be part of the solution.

Market Failure, Government Failure, or Organizational Failure?

Interestingly, most of the factors that are regarded as causes of the recent crisis in Korea were once presented as the sources of its economic success. Kim (1997a: 241) put it (see also Miller, 1990) this way:

> The fabled Icarus [in Greek mythology] had powerful artificial wings that enabled him to fly so high, so close to the sun, that the wax wings melted and he plunged to his death. The paradox is that one's greatest asset can later become one's most serious liability. The same paradox applies to many aspects of Korea's experience.

In this section, we give further explanation to these issues. Under the assumption of widespread market failure during the initial development phase, governments and organizations took initiatives and Korea experienced successes. However, now Korean industry is affected by both government and organizational failure. Williamson's (1975) 'market failures' framework argues that organizations are superior to markets in managing complex and uncertain economic transactions because (and to the extent that) they reduce 'transaction costs'. Speaking figuratively, the government played the role of an organization. Because market forces were inefficient in driving economic development in the NIEs (Sharma, 1985), government organization outperformed market functions. The question then becomes: when does the government become inefficient? As Kim (1997a) points out, the government played a critical role as a facilitator in the electronics industry during the early stages of its development, but in highly dynamic sectors such as semiconductors it was unable to play a decisive role. Rather, the large conglomerates took the initiatives. Leipziger (1988: 131) provided some possible 'decision rules' for intervention:

> The decision process might involve the following series of steps: (a) an assessment of the direct and indirect costs to society of the distressed industry's performance, that is, a judgment of the extent of

externalities (*the 'intervention test'*); (b) an analysis of the source of decline and a judgment on its reversibility (*the 'reversibility test'*); and (c) if a public solution is needed, realistic near-term and medium-term objectives should be placed on both the duration and cost of intervention (*the 'efficiency test'*) ... The intervention should be monitored vis-à-vis its public objectives (*the 'monitorability test'*) and potentially reversed or abandoned if it fails to measure up.

However, recent public policy seems to be based more on *ad hoc* actions rather than long term direction. Furthermore, this kind of inconsistency of policies, and the lack of a coherent economic philosophy, actually made things worse. It seems that the balance between free market and intervention has not been wisely pursued. Sometimes the 'let alone' policy was directly regarded as the market-orientated policy. At other times direct control by the 'visible hand' was viewed as necessary intervention. The government became a major obstacle to market mechanisms, which, it may be argued, have now become more efficient under dynamic and globalized industrial world conditions. Here we see a typical 'government failure' phenomenon.

What about organizational failure? The *chaebols* and entrepreneurship were needed to contribute to catch-up. Under environmental uncertainty, firms built their capabilities through internalization and diversification on the assumption of market failure. Large conglomerates were needed for efficient technology transfer. The *chaebols* were also able to more readily obtain (with state help) needed and requisite financial resources. However, this 'big is better' approach continued after its merits were less apparent, and needed to be better counterbalanced with a 'small is beautiful' view. There are also several particular characteristics of such concentration of economic activity in conglomerates worthy of exploration. Choi (1996) characterized the *chaebols* as having family centred ownership and control, including real power over the general meeting of stockholders, and a low capital ratio to total company assets. First is the matter of family ownership. According to the Fair Trade Commission of Korea, in 1996 the 'Big Five' *chaebols* (except Daewoo) had about 40–50 affiliated companies. As of 1995, the numbers of affiliated firms were 46 in Hyundai, 55 in Samsung, 48 in LG, 25 in Daewoo and 32 in SK (Choi, 1996). They also averaged 140 different businesses apiece (*The Economist*, 1997). Since most Korean *chaebols* are family driven, family members are significant shareholders in many of the subsidiaries. For the Big Five, between 1990 and 1994, the head of the company and their family held, on average, about 13 per cent of total shares (Fair Trade Commission data). In addition, the shares held by the affiliated subsidiaries of each *chaebol* amounted to about 37 per cent. Therefore, the total shares held by the head, family and subsidiaries accounted for about 50 per cent on average.

Second, the head's absolute power over the company and the general stockholder meeting is important. Choi (1996) reported that those representing only about 64 per cent of the total shares issued attended such meetings. Small stockholders were not interested in influencing decision making, but rather in marginal profits from stock market quotations. Therefore, the head and family easily held real power over such meetings. Accordingly, the corporate governance systems in the *chaebols* lacked 'checks and balances'. They seemingly practised the separation of ownership and management, but in reality it was not fully so. For instance, the head actually designates the Chief Executive Officer. The supervisory functions of financial institutions over companies have also been very weak. In addition, traditional Korean 'managerial style' can be characterized as 'militaristic' or authoritarian and paternalistic (Lee and You, 1987: 75; Steers *et al.*, 1989; Chung *et al.*, 1997). It may be argued that top management's absolute power over the company and employees may be efficient under stable environments. However, under higher environmental uncertainty, 'the cost of maintaining a company without flocking and innovation, where every adaptation had to be ordered from the highest levels of the hierarchy, was too great' (Geus, 1997: 140). Geus used the term 'flocking'[1] to emphasize the importance of working together for rapid learning and innovation and social propagation. Thus, 'freedom and tolerance are necessary to increase the learning abilities of the organisation' (ibid.: 152). This centralization also appeared in international management. Kim raises this problem when observing that there are centralized interactions between the headquarters and foreign subsidiaries of MNCs (contributions to Slater and Strange, 1997, include analysis of internationalization and control strategies of Korean companies). Therefore, greater empowerment and decentralization need to be enhanced in the *chaebols*.

   Third, a weak financial structure that lacks transparency is increasingly apparent. According to Fair Trade Commission statistics, the average debt of the top 30 *chaebols* exceeded their own capital by four times as of 1 April 1997.[2] Their own capital ratio (capital ratio to company assets) was 20.6 per cent (thus, about 80 per cent came from the banks). Internally held shares (by the head, family and subsidiaries through mutual investment) accounted for 43 per cent of shares. The biggest *chaebols* held a combined total of Won 6.7 trillion (about US$ 3.9 billion) in intersubsidiary (or cross) payment guarantees, a figure that exceeds their total equity capital as of the end of April 1997. Even more worrying, as *chaebol* affiliates guarantee each other's debts, but do not produce consolidated accounts, debts are grossly understated and opaqueness enhanced. Yet, when exports slump and a currency tumbles, companies can no longer service foreign debts. Furthermore, Korean firms (like their Japanese rivals) have long used property as the main collateral for their borrowings, but 'property booms' burst and prices then collapse (*The Economist*, 1997).

   With these characteristics, there are striking structural problems and weaknesses associated with *chaebol* dominated environments. For example, the *chaebols* were dependent upon the Japanese for parts and components because initially there were few qualified indigenous suppliers (Castley;

Kim, 1997a). Now reasons for continuing dependence include short product life cycles and the inadequate upgrading abilities of local subcontractors (Bloom, 1992). This in turn partly comes from exclusive relationships between *chaebols* and suppliers; and the former's insufficient technical support for the latter. Consequently, the growth of production and exports in the Korean electronics industry brought the vicious trade deficit in electronics with Japan (Castley). The emergence and development of dynamic and innovative small and medium-sized enterprises (SMEs) was also stunted, a situation exacerbated by 'financial repression' (Cathie) limiting favourable loans to them.

All these factors together reveal the properties of 'organization failure'. First of all, reducing 'transaction costs' may lead to an increase of 'coordination costs'. Large conglomerates with high structural differentiation are liable to have the formation of 'subcultures', which makes it difficult to coordinate across units and eventually leads to higher coordination costs (Lawrence and Lorsch, 1967; Jermier *et al.*, 1991; Dougherty, 1992). Another feature of organization failure is related to organizational inertia. The *chaebols* showed the inertial properties of organizations (Kim; Samsung Group, 1994). The conservative forces of history and tradition are one of the many commonly noted constraints upon change in organizations (Hannan and Freeman, 1977). It may be argued that under higher environmental uncertainty, organizational inertia becomes 'a liability rather than an asset', preventing organizations from changing with enough scope and speed (Scott, 1992). Given these properties of government and organization failure, and under the recent financial crisis, is it still possible for the Korean model of industrialization to demonstrate its capabilities? We return to these issues in our Conclusion to this volume.

THE KOREAN MODEL: SUSTAINABLE, OR JUST A MIRAGE?

The Korean model has been challenged severely by both internal and external forces. Can the Korean model survive the recent troubles? Or will it be an 'Asian Tiger', previously one of the most robust and seemingly full of vitality, that continues to be attacked by serious illness and laid low? Previous writers argued that Korean industrialization could be a role model for 'late-latecomers' (Amsden, 1989). Shortening the time period of industrialization and standing as a global player in electronics (especially semiconductor parts) clearly demonstrates the accomplishments. What are some future tasks that Korean companies should undertake? The imminent hurdle to jump is, needless to say, the financial crisis. For the government side, it should formulate consistent policies, become less *dirigiste* and draw back from unnecessary interventions. The *chaebols* should undertake their structural reformations to enhance managerial and financial transparency. Finally, but not least, labour will be faced with mass unemployment by the legalization of layoffs, which had previously been virtually impossible in Korea (see Bae *et al.*, 1997). This labour market flexibility issue needs to be resolved in the context of production upgrading (Rowley and Lewis, 1996).

There are at least three different views on the recent crisis. The most optimistic view regards it as just a matter of US dollar liquidity, which can be resolved, albeit with difficulty, in time and is thus not a grave problem. Another perspective argues that the heart of the crisis lies in the Korean model of industrialization and economic growth. An intermediate view holds that the Korean model was correct, but that governments and institutions simply failed to adjust to changing environments. Therefore, the economy should be able to regain its prior status if restructuring programmes are successfully carried out. As a result, many Koreans regard the crisis as 'God's blessing in disguise', which will force changes that will help the economy prosper once again. Regardless of the position one takes, two imminent challenges remain: the restructuring of the *chaebols*, and enhancing labour market flexibility. Resolution of the crisis is highly dependent upon simultaneously successfully tackling these twin challenges. We return to these in our concluding contribution.

In many ways, Korean business and management stands at a crossroads. Many of the problems that have been noted, predicted, talked about and tracked for so long are now all too apparent and visible. This does not mean that the future scenario for Korea is wholly negative. There have been great successes and cause for genuine pride. The country has moved from a poor, underdeveloped and authoritarian state to enjoy rapid economic growth and exports, becoming more prosperous and publicly courted as an investor and job generator as well as enjoying greater democracy. For instance, the economy has grown at an average of 8.6 per cent over the last three decades; exports ballooned from just US$ 33 million in 1960 to a massive US$ 130 billion by 1996 as Korea became the world's largest producer of ships and memory chips, the fifth largest car maker and the eleventh largest economy (*The Economist*, 1997). Korean per capita income exploded from just US$ 146 in 1950 to almost US$ 11,000 in 1997 (Cathie) (though it is still a 'poor relation' among OECD counties save for Mexico and Turkey). Nevertheless, the interlinked problems of a *dirigiste* economy, intimate government– finance–business nexus and relationships, sclerotic *chaebols* and labour flexibility have to be resolved. This does not mean that future developments must follow the previous pattern. While we need to remember economies may not grow fast forever, 'Made in Korea' will continue to attract the custom of international markets and its successes a band (albeit smaller in number) of admirers. 'Icarus' may well have flown too close to the sun, but the 'wings' can be rebuilt to fly again.

ACKNOWLEDGEMENTS

Our thanks to Robert Fitzgerald for his perceptive lexical points and to Outi Aarnio for enhancing our economic clarity. The normal disclaimers apply.

NOTES

1. From now on, undated author references relate to the authors' contributions in this volume.
2. However, so have Japan and Germany. Thanks to Robert Fitzgerald for this point.
3. A significant and important debate, whose detailed analysis is beyond the scope of this contribution, is worthy of note here. For several commentators, such as some economists, 'competitiveness' is meaningless when applied to national economies (Krugman, 1994a). Also, competitiveness is not an unambiguous concept. For example, in the short run it can be maintained simply by devaluation, and this has nothing to do with technological capabilities. See whole issue of *Oxford Review of Economic Policy* (1996) on competitiveness and Boltho's (1996) assessment. This includes the view that the international competitiveness of a country can be equated with the 'real' (an index of relative unit labour costs in a common currency) exchange rate and that improvements in competitiveness involve declines in real exchange rates from falls in 'nominal' exchange rates. Krugman (1996) sees the discussion of 'national competitiveness' as dangerous as it implies nations competing against each other, whereas international trade is not a zero-sum game in which somebody must always lose. He outlines 'schools' and views on competitiveness and international trade (mercantilist, classicist, strategist, realist) and ideas and implications of 'comparative advantage' and 'general equilibrium' in this area. He sceptically concludes that the interest in competitiveness, and the debate it has fermented, 'is simply a matter of time-honoured fallacies about international trade being dressed up in new and pretentious rhetoric' (ibid.: 24). Many thanks to Outi Aarnio for bringing this to our attention.
4. From now on, 'Korea' is used as shorthand for South Korea.
5. Endogenous growth models typically analyse precisely technological transfer from abroad, and 'learning by doing', but do not specify the source of technological change (it occurs at an exogenously given rate).
6. This is whereby Korea imports from Japan then exports to the US. The Japanese initially preferred this pattern (Castley).
7. There is a wealth of literature in this area. This includes the area of flexible specialization and its effect on competitiveness, which is beyond the scope of this Introduction. See, *inter alia*, Sabel and Zeitlin, 1997; Storper and Salais, 1997.
8. However, in 1996 the net sales of SEC decreased from US$ 19.2 billion in 1995 to US$ 18.8 billion, mainly due to a sharp slide in DRAM prices that began its downward swing from the second quarter of 1996 worldwide. In that same year, semiconductor related sales decreased by 31.8 per cent.
9. By 1998, SEC, LGE and Hyundai Electronics supplied 40 per cent of the world's DRAM memory chips (*Financial Times*, 1998), however, it is a different story in the non-memory area. SEC fell behind foreign competitors in non-memory devices, which constitute a much greater share of the world's semiconductor chip market (Kim, 1997b).
10. The IMF recommended that all domestic banks meet the 8 per cent capital adequacy ratio requested by the Bank for International Settlements after reflecting 100 per cent of their appraisal losses to the fiscal balance by the end of March 1998.
11. The term is taken from the story of the titmouse. The titmouse learned faster, increased its chances of survival and evolved more quickly, because it 'flocked'.
12. The top 30 *chaebols'* average debt–equity ratio of 400 per cent compared with the US average of 70 per cent (*The Economist*, 1998).

REFERENCES

Amsden, A.H. (1989) *Asia's Next Giant: South Korea and Late Industrialization*. New York and Oxford: Oxford University Press.

Applebaum, R. and Henderson, J. (eds) (1992) *States and Development in the Asian Pacific Rim*. London: Sage.

Bae, J., Rowley, C., Kim, D.-H. and Lawler, J. (1997) 'Korean Industrial Relations at the Crossroads: The Recent Labour Troubles', *Asia Pacific Business Review*, Vol. 3, No. 3, pp. 148–60.

Bloom, M. (1992) *Technological Change in the Korean Electronics Industry*. Paris: Development Centre of the OECD.

Boltho, A. (1996) 'The Assessment: International Competitiveness', *Oxford Review of Economic Policy*, Vol. 1, No. 3, pp. 1–16.

Castley, R.J. (1997) *Korea's Economic Miracle: The Crucial Role of Japan.* London: Macmillan.

Cho, D.-S. (1994) 'A Dynamic Approach to International Competitiveness: The Case of Korea', *Journal of Far Eastern Business*, Vol. 1, No. 1, pp. 17–36.

Choi, J. (1996) *Sunjinhwa-rul wihan Chaebol-eui Suntaek (The Chaebol's Choice for the Advancement).* Seoul: GoWon.

Chung; K.H., Lee, H.C. and Jung, K.H. (1997) *Korean Management: Global Strategy and Cultural Transformation.* Berlin: de Gruyter.

Cohen, W.M. and Levinthal, D.A. (1990) 'Absorptive Capacity: A New Perspective on Learning and Innovation', *Administrative Science Quarterly*, Vol. 35, No. 1, pp.128–52.

Dougherty, D. (1992) 'Interpretive Barriers to Successful Product Innovation in Large Firms', *Organization Science*, Vol. 3, pp. 179–202.

Dunlop, J. (1958) *Industrial Relations Systems.* New York: Henry Holt and Company.

Economist, The (1997) 'South Korea: The End of the Miracle', 29 November, pp. 25–7.

Economist, The (1998) 'East Asia Economic Survey: Frozen Miracle', 7 March, pp.1–20.

Ernst, D. and O'Connor, D. (1992) *Competing in the Electronics Industry: The Experience of Newly Industrialising Economies.* Paris: Development Centre of the OECD.

Financial Times (1998), 'Hyundai halts production of chips to ease glut', 4 June, p.27.

Fitzgerald, R. (1994) 'The Competitive Advantages of Far Eastern Businesses', *Journal of Far Eastern Business*, Vol. 1, No. 1.

Garvin, D.A. (1993) 'Building a Learning Organization', *Harvard Business Review*, July-Aug., pp. 78–91.

Geus, Aris de (1997) *The Living Company.* Boston, MA: Harvard Business School Press.

Hannan, M.T. and Freeman, J. (1977) 'The Population Ecology of Organizations', *American Journal of Sociology*, Vol. 82, pp. 929–64.

Jermier, J.M., Slocum, J.W., Jr, Fry, L.W. and Gaines, J. (1991) 'Organizational Subcultures in a Soft Bureaucracy: Resistance behind the Myth and Facade of an Official Culture', *Organization Science*, Vol. 2, pp. 170–94.

Kennedy, P. (1987) *The Rise and Fall of the Great Powers.* Lexington, MA: Lexington Books.

Kim, L. (1997a) *Imitation to Innovation: The Dynamics of Korea's Technological Learning.* Boston, MA: Harvard Business School Press.

Kim, L. (1997b) 'The Dynamics of Samsung's Technological Learning in Semiconductors', *California Management Review*, Vol. 39, No. 3, pp. 86–100.

Kogut, B. (1993) 'Introduction', in B. Kogut (ed.), *Country Competitiveness: Technology and the Organizing of Work.* New York, NY: Oxford University Press, pp. 3–12.

Koo, H. (1987) 'The Interplay of State, Society, Class and the World System in East Asian Development: The Cases of Korea and Taiwan', in F.C. Deyo (ed.), *The Political Economy of the New Asian Industialization.* Ithaca, NY: Cornell University Press, pp. 165–81.

Krugman, P.R. (1994a) 'Competitiveness: A Dangerous Obsession', *Foreign Affairs*, Vol. 73, No. 2, pp. 28–44.

Krugman, P.R. (1994b) 'The Myth of Asia's Miracle', *Foreign Affairs*, Vol. 73, No. 6, pp. 62–78.

Krugman, P.R. (1996) 'Making Sense of the Competitiveness Debate', *Oxford Review of Economic Policy*, Vol. 12, No. 3, pp. 17–25.

Lau, L.J. (ed.) (1990) *Models of Economic Development: A Comparative History of Economic Growth in South Korea and Taiwan.* San Francisco, CA: ICS Press.

Lawrence, P.R and Lorsch, J.W. (1967) *Organization and Environment.* Boston, MA: Harvard University Press.

Lazonick, W. (1991) *Business Organization and the Myth of the Market Economy.* New York, NY: Cambridge University Press.

Lee, S.M. and Sangjin, Y. (1987) 'The K-Type Management: A Driving Force of Korean Prosperity', *Management International Review*, Vol. 27, No. 4, pp. 68–77.

Leipziger, D.M. (1988) 'Industrial Restructuring in Korea', *World Development*, Vol. 16, No. 1, pp. 121–35.

McDermott, M. (1992) 'The Internationalization of the South Korean and Taiwanese Electronics Industries: The European Dimension', in S. Young and J. Hamill (eds), *Europe and the Multinationals: Issues and Responses for the 1990s.* Aldershot: Elgar, pp. 206–31.

Miller, D. (1990) *The Icarus Paradox: How Exceptional Companies Bring about Their Own Downfall.* New York, NY: Harper Business.

Nonaka, I. (1994) 'The Knowledge-Creating Company', *Harvard Business Review*, Nov.-Dec., pp. 96–104.

Moore, L.F. and Jennings, D.P (1995) *Human Resource Management on the Pacific Rim: Institutions, Practices and Attitudes.* Berlin: de Gruyter.

Oxford Review of Economic Policy (1996) 'International Competitiveness', Vol. 12, No. 3.

Piore, M. and Sabel, C. (1984) *The Second Industrial Divide: Prospects for Prosperity.* New York, NY: Basic Books.

Porter, M.E. (1990) *The Competitive Advantage of Nations.* New York, NY: The Free Press.

Redding, G.S. (1990) *The Spirit of Chinese Capitalism.* Berlin: de Gruyter.

Rodrick, D. (1998) *Controversies, Institutions and Economic Performance in East Asia*, NBER Working Paper, No. 5914.

Rowley, C. (1994) 'The Illusion of Flexible Specialisation: The Case of the British Ceramics Industry', *New Technology, Work and Employment*, Vol. 4, No. 2, pp. 127–39.

Rowley, C. (1996) 'Flexible Specialisation: Some Comparative Dimensions and Evidence from the Ceramic Tile Industry', *New Technology, Work and Employment*, Vol. 11, No. 2, pp. 125–36.

Rowley, C. (1998a) 'Manufacturing Mobility? Internationalization, Change and Continuity', *Journal of General Management*, Vol. 23, No. 3, pp. 21–34.

Rowley, C. (ed.) (1998b) *HRM in the Asia Pacific: Convergence Questioned.* London and Portland OR: Frank Cass.

Rowley, C. and Lewis, M. (1996) 'Greater China at the Crossroads? Convergence, Culture and Competitiveness', *Asia Pacific Business Review*, Vol. 2, No. 3, pp. 1–22.

Sabel, C. and Zeitlin, J. (eds) (1997) *Worlds of Possibilities: Flexibility and Mass Production in Western Industrialization.* Cambridge: Cambridge University Press.

Samsung Electronics (1996) *Annual Report: Global Vision in the 21st Century.* Seoul: Samsung Electronics.

Samsung Group (1994) *Samsung's New Management.* Seoul: Samsung Printing Co.

Scott, W.R. (1992) *Organizations: Rational, Natural, and Open Systems*, 3rd edn. Englewood Cliffs, NJ: Prentice Hall.

Senge, P.M. (1990) *The Fifth Discipline.* New York, NY: Doubleday.

Sharma, B. (1985) *Aspects of Industrial Relations in ASEAN.* Singapore: Institute of Southeast Asian Studies.

Slater, J. and Strange, R. (eds) (1997) *Business Relationships with East Asia.* London: Routledge.

Steers, R.M., Shin, Y.K. and Ungson, G.R. (1989) *The Chaebol: Korea's New Industrial Might.* New York, NY: Harper and Row.

Storper, M. and Salais, R. (1997) *Worlds of Production: The Action Framework of the Economy.* Cambridge, MA: Harvard University Press.

Thompson, J.D. (1967) *Organizations in Action.* New York, NY: McGraw-Hill.

Utterback, J.M. (1994) *Mastering the Dynamics of Innovation: How Companies Can Seize Opportunities in the Face of Technological Change.* Cambridge, MA: Harvard University Press.

Vernon, R. (1966) 'International Investment and International Trade in the Product Cycle', *Quarterly Journal of Economics*, Vol. 80, pp. 190–207.

Vernon, R. (1979) 'The Product Life Cycle Hypothesis in a New Industrial Environment', *Bulletin of Economics and Statistics*, Vol. 41, pp. 265–7.

Westphal, L.E. (1982) 'The Private Sector as "Principal Engine" of Development: Korea', *Finance and Development*, Vol. 19, pp. 34–8.

Whitley, R. (1992) *Business Systems in East Asian Firms: Firms, Markets and Societies.* London: Sage.

Williamson, O.E. (1975) *Markets and Hierarchies: Analysis and Antitrust Implications.* New York: The Free Press.

World Bank (1993) *The East Asian Miracle: Economic Growth and Public Policy.* Oxford: Oxford University Press.

World Development (1988), Vol. 16, No. 1.

Zysman, J. (1983) *Governments, Markets and Growth.* Oxford: Martin Robertson.

Financial Contagion in East Asia and the Origins of the Economic and Financial Crisis in Korea

JOHN CATHIE

The last quarter of 1997 saw the spread of a financial contagion in Asia, which has come to undermine the economic performance and possibly the political stability of a significant number of the ten eastern countries of the region (China,[1] Hong Kong, Indonesia, Japan, South Korea,[2] Malaysia, the Philippines, Singapore, Taiwan and Thailand). The financial and economic crisis of 1997–98 in Asia has not only affected the region itself, but threatens the prospects of economic growth in the world economy, which may in turn result in a recession on a global scale. The crisis in the region has also in a spectacular fashion seen the largest financial rescue packages put in place (in Korea and Indonesia) for any single country by the International Monetary Fund (IMF) since its establishment in the 1940s (Fisher, 1998). These rescue packages have been subject to considerable difficulty, as the countries concerned have been reluctant to accept the 'conditionalities' that the IMF has required for their financial support. The reform of Korea's and Indonesia's economic policies goes to the heart of their respective development models, requiring a complete overhaul of strategies that have hitherto accompanied their highly successful growth achievements.

Since the 1960s these Asian countries have become richer than any other region of the world economy. In per capita terms the Philippines grew at two per cent per annum, while China, Indonesia, Japan, Malaysia and Thailand achieved growth rates of three to five per cent per annum. However, the annual growth rates of the four 'Tiger' or 'Dragon' economies (Hong Kong, Korea, Singapore, Taiwan) over a sustained 30 year period were well in excess of six per cent. This growth performance has attracted epithets of 'exemplary', 'amazing', 'miraculous', 'spectacular', and it has also been accompanied by an intense academic debate as to the causes of the Asian economic miracle. The year 1997 may well be a watershed for the region where continuous and positive economic growth becomes elusive for some of the hitherto hyper-growth economies, as regional competition intensifies in the wake of competitive currency devaluations.

John Cathie, University of Cambridge.

THE ASIAN ECONOMIC MODEL?

The Asian economic model in the form of the economic policies adopted in Japan, Taiwan or Korea were seen by some in the West as offering lessons for improving the performance of rich countries themselves, as well as offering policy lessons for developing countries (see, *inter alia*, Wilkinson, 1994). For some time Japanese management practice was also considered as superior to that of the West, having lessons to teach (see, *inter alia*, Stewart, 1996; Rowley, 1997). In a similar fashion, it was argued that Asian state-promoted industrial policy offered lessons on industrial organization for the West. The Asian model was said to represent a combination of free market economics, traditional family values in contrast to Western social welfare programmes, and of hard work and thrift, authoritarian politics and a strong emphasis on education.

The idea of 'Asian values' as the source of Asian prosperity has been advocated by, among others, the Prime Minister of Malaysia, Mohamad Mahathir, as the reason for the success of the Asian economic model. While the Asian region has been drawn into financial contagion and currency instability, the factors that affect each of the countries in crisis are different in each country case, and the macroeconomic stabilization policies required for individual counties are materially different. The Asian contagion has different causes requiring different country responses, with some Asian economies likely to stabilize quicker than others, and with lesser social costs. The idea of a common Asian economic model in the light of the financial crisis seems now to have been overstated all along: whereas there are common factors that have contributed to the economic success of the area, there are also profound differences among the countries in the region.

The East Asian economic growth experience since the 1960s, particularly the performance of the Tiger economies, has produced a vast academic literature as to the nature and causes of this exemplary phenomenon. In the analysis of such economies, economic performance has come to concentrate upon three distinctive issues in the debate (Sarel, 1996). The first of these issues is on the nature of economic growth in the region, particularly whether this can be attributed to 'factor accumulation', or to 'technological progress'. The traditional economic view would hold that sustained economic progress can only be achieved through technological progress (Solow, 1956). This intensive economic growth suggests a continuous technological improvement as the basis of economic growth in the Tiger economies. However, the extensive economic growth hypothesis has been proposed as an explanation of the Tiger experience and has emphasized the accumulation of labour and capital, rather than that of gains in efficiency as such (Krugman, 1994). This thesis undermines the notion of a 'miraculous' Asian model if growth is explained by the accumulation of capital and labour alone. It also suggests that the high growth path cannot be sustained in the long run. Empirical evidence does suggest that accumulation of capital and labour have played a significant part in the East Asian experience (Kim and Lau, 1994).

The second issue, which has perhaps caused the greatest controversy, is that of the role of the state, or of public policy, as the explanation for the Asian economic miracle (Rodrik, 1994). In this debate three strands of opinion are evident: (a) that the free market has operated in an essentially neoclassical fashion allowing the efficiency of markets, and thus an exemplary growth performance, in Asia; (b) that public policy has been selectively interventionist, particularly in regard to the promotion of industrialization, and this explains the Asian miracle; (c) an agnostic view with regard to the free market and interventionist explanations. This last view (c) holds that analysis of individual Asian economic success is subject to a selection bias, and that counterfactual propositions are not considered, and perhaps more telling, that public policy in the Tiger economies has not been homogeneous. Thus, Japan and Korea have followed highly interventionist policies, whereas Hong Kong and Thailand have not; redistributive policies have been followed in Malaysia, but not elsewhere. Clientelism has predominated in Indonesia and Thailand. Strong states, some authoritarian, are evident, as in Korea and Singapore. Japan and Korea have conglomerates, while Taiwan has small entrepreneurial firms. The role of education in these economies and its contribution to their economic success is not easily determined, particularly the direction of causation: has education brought growth or growth brought education? Arguments that characterize the exceptional growth experience in the Tiger economies as attributable either to the market or the state do not fully capture or explain the Asian model, since there are elements of both in many country experiences.

The third issue has considered investment and exports as the engines of economic growth in East Asia, particularly in the Tiger economies. Empirically, rates of savings and investment in these economies have been exceptionally high during the 30 year period, especially as the 'take-off' gathered pace. These economies have been open in so far as they have placed a high priority upon exporting in world markets, which has in turn exposed them to foreign technology and competition in these markets and rapid technological progress.

In sum, it seems that generalizations about the Asian economic model and the causes of the Tiger growth miracle are unlikely to offer a full explanation for the individual growth experiences. These are better understood in the context of country analysis; not only the variations in the conduct of their macroeconomic policy, but also their microeconomic policies and their cultural, institutional and national circumstances and experiences. This, in turn, must limit any overarching and all-encompassing explanations (and prescriptive panaceas).

The Asian financial contagion has not affected all the Tiger economies to the same degree, with Taiwan being able to withstand the financial pressures from currency markets (because of massive foreign exchange reserves), while Hong Kong for the moment (with the reserves of the Bank of China) can maintain the peg with the US dollar. Singapore is less well positioned, and Korea is in the most vulnerable position of the Tigers since currency reserves are all but depleted. Overall, it seems that Indonesia is in a position of greatest currency weakness, as witnessed by a currency devaluation of 75 per cent of its value in a matter of weeks in early 1998.

THE ASIAN MONETARY CRISIS

The immediate causes of the currency crisis are complex but can be located in 1994 when China effectively devalued its currency by some 40 per cent and the Japanese Yen depreciated by some 25 per cent (Bergsten, 1997; Liu et al., 1998). The sharp decline in these two key currencies in the region caused intense competitive pressure on the countries in the rest of Asia and altered their trade positions such that large deficits resulted in South East Asia, particularly in Indonesia, Korea and Thailand. The crisis broke in 1995 when markets began to doubt the sustainability of these Asian economies as their domestic financial systems began to indicate weaknesses in the form of unsustainable debt, overinvestment and unsustainable growth targets. The devaluations in Japan and China might not have been translated into a contagion had Taiwan not chosen to devalue also, since it had enjoyed a strong trade surplus, four per cent of gross domestic product (GDP), strong economic growth and the third largest currency reserves (US$ 100 billion) in the world. Therefore, it did not have an economic need to devalue. Its action in turn put considerable pressure upon Hong Kong and threatened its economic stability. Taiwan had opted for an economic policy of competitive devaluation not dissimilar to that widely practised in the world economy of the 1930s.

While Hong Kong has managed to maintain its peg with the US dollar, Thailand, Singapore, Indonesia and Malaysia were unable to withstand currency pressure. As the contagion took hold in the region, finally Korea was drawn into the regional devaluations with a spectacular collapse of the Korean Won. The Won fell in value by some 50 per cent at the end of 1997 and the stock market followed by dropping some 60 per cent. Thailand, Indonesia and Korea were forced by economic collapse to negotiate rescue packages with the IMF in an attempt to stabilize their respective economies. The IMF packages have called into question the Asian model and in particular the 'Korean Model'. The Managing Director of the IMF, Michel Camdessus, urged the Koreans to start again, by abolishing the industrial conglomerates, the *chaebols*, which lie at the very heart of the Korean development model. Camdessus, using a literary metaphor from the Spanish poet Miquel de Unamuno (who 'used his ideas as he did his boots; he wore them out and then threw them away'), urged Korea to scrap its development model and begin afresh.

THE ORIGINS AND CAUSES OF THE CRISIS IN KOREA

Korea has achieved an incredible rate of economic growth in the relatively short period of a generation (see Chung *et al.*, 1997). In 1950, Korea was among the poorest countries in the world with a per capita income of some US$ 146, yet by 1997 this figure had grown to US$ 10,973. In this period, Korea had come from being regarded as a 'basket case' to become the newest member of the OECD in 1996, with ambitions to outperform Japan by overtaking its economic position in the new millennium. The success of the Korean industrial economy was such that in 1996 it was the first supplier of computer memory chips, the second largest shipbuilder in the world, the third largest producer of semiconductors, the fourth largest maker of electronics, the fifth largest car maker, and the largest steel producer. For a country with a population of 45 million and few natural resources this industrial performance does indeed seem to be aptly described as 'miraculous'.

Korean GDP grew by an average of nine per cent in the 1960s, 9.3 per cent in the 1970s, and in the 1980s and 1990s by nearly ten per cent. Korea had been subjugated by Japan from 1910 to 1945 in what can only be described as a brutal colonization, during which Korean identity had been suppressed and the colony was treated as a 'rice bowl' by its colonial masters. From 1950 to 1953 a civil war divided the country and more than a million Koreans died, five million were refugees (25 per cent of the population), agricultural production nearly collapsed, gross national product (GNP) dropped 14 per cent, and basic infrastructure, including US$ 2 billion property damage, was devastated (Cathie, 1989). In 1994, when Korea became a lender to developing countries and was about to graduate to the twelfth largest economy in the world, the World Bank Vice-President for East Asia referred enthusiastically to the Korean model as an example to the developing world (*The Economist*, 1995).

The causes of the Korean economic miracle and the ingredients of its model of development have been attributed to a number of general factors. These include those listed in Table 1.

TABLE 1
INGREDIENTS OF THE KOREAN DEVELOPMENT MODEL

- Infusion of US economic aid (mostly grants) in early period of development
- Literate and well trained workforce – industrious, disciplined and compliant
- Emergence of a group of entrepreneurs
- Unusually effective cooperation between government and business
- Industrial conglomerates not dissimilar to Japanese *ziabatsu* or *Sogo Shoushabut*
- Authoritarian political regime (for most of 1950–88) totally committed to economic growth directing the economy to this single minded goal – Park Chung Hee (1961–79) was regarded as the classic 'benevolent dictator'
- Confucian heritage
- Legacy of the Japanese occupation
- *Laissez faire* economic policies, or at least an adherence to achieving economic growth on world markets by exporting
- Protection and military support from the US as a frontier state during the Cold War, particularly the fear of North Korea and the need to build a strong economic, as well as a military, state

Korean economic growth was firmly established in 1961 when Park Chung Hee took over as head of state. From 1953 until 1961 the development strategy had been preoccupied with post-civil war reconstruction, and for a short period had considered agricultural development as the primary focus of its development efforts. The macroeconomic policy pursued during this period was characterized by massive economic aid from the US, supporting the government budget, and attempts to stabilize the Won, usually through successive devaluations. Stabilization programmes saw cuts in growth and investment, culminating in the resignation of President Rhee in the wake of student riots. General Park took over in a military coup and the first development plan saw exports massively double in just 18 months.

The Korean development model could be aptly described as the 'Park Development Model', since from 1961 until his assassination in 1979 his authoritarian and single-minded approach to economic growth and development dominated the country. Indeed, the problems that his approach to economic policy has bequeathed to the economy lie at the heart of the current economic crisis in Korea. The IMF rescue package requires the total dismantling of the vestiges of the Park legacy, particularly in the area of the financial liberalization of the economy and the role of the *chaebol* in the economy. The strength of the Park model lay in its capacity to mobilize resources for the primary development objective of industrialization on a massive scale and sustained economic growth. Annual growth targets were set in successive development plans and these targets were usually achieved in the planning period. Park had been educated in Japanese military academies and as a member of the 'class of the 8th' modelled the Korean economy on the Japanese development model, albeit with distinctive Korean characteristics.

THE *CHAEBOLS*

The building of an industrial economy was undertaken by the promotion of industrial conglomerates known as *chaebols* (literally, 'big money') that worked closely with the state in their pursuit of industrial and economic growth goals (see Chung *et al.*, 1997). In a classic fashion Korean industrial development began with the textile industry exporting on world markets. Industrial policy progressed from light industry during this period to heavy industry, including shipbuilding and steel production, and in the 1970s and 1980s moved on to car production and electronics, including microchips and state of the art technological production (see other contributions to this volume). The industrial strategy involved higher quality and higher value-added industrial production. The Economic Planning Board in the presidential palace (the Blue House) met weekly with the heads of the *chaebols* to plan and coordinate national industrial and economic growth objectives, with the state essentially setting these economic targets. The macroeconomy was single mindedly adjusted to these objectives without regard to other considerations. Labour policy was conducted with a ruthless suppression of trade unions and the use of the army to settle labour disputes. In the 1980s the law recognized the rights of workers to secure employment; however, wages were determined by the *chaebols* backed by the full force of the state (see Bae *et al.*, 1997). Real wages did remain constant for much of the Park period, though in the 1970s they began to rise steadily.

Many of the *chaebols* came into existence in the 1950s and 1960s, taking up US construction contracts under the American aid programme. They diversified as the industrial policy of the government of Korea evolved from light industry, through heavy industry to high technology industrial output. Korean government economic policy encouraged industrial concentration in such conglomerates as the means of achieving the societal goal of development through selling industrial production on world markets.

The real and the financial economies were totally committed to this end, and policy was designed to accomplish this. Failures of strategy by the *chaebols*, such as those investment projects in construction in the Middle East in the early 1970s, were written off. The losses were, thus, absorbed by the Korean economy and people as a necessary part of achieving economic prosperity. The single-minded pursuit of economic growth by governments undoubtedly explains much of the success of the economic model in achieving exceptional performance. However, the costs of policy failure were borne by society when the industrial strategy faltered, or as it did in some circumstances, failed.

POLICY LOANS AND THE BANKING SYSTEM

While the *chaebols* provided the form of industrial organization that formed the core of the Korean development model, the state provided these organizations with their production objectives, urging them to expand into new lines of production that met the overall industrial strategy of the country. The *chaebols* that responded to the overall strategy were rewarded by the state with 'policy loans'. These policy loans were in effect cheap sources of loanable funds for these companies. In the 1970s, some 60 per cent of Korean bank lending was in the form of such policy loans (*The Economist*, 1995). State intervention also took an excessive form. For example, some 120 documents were required to export a product. Similarly, in the early 1970s the Daewoo *chaebol* was specializing in textiles but was ordered to take over a machine-tool maker and a shipyard as well as to develop a motor car. This resulted in a debt/equity ratio of some 900 per cent, and when the oil shock hit the economy the government had to rescue the group. Government policy under Park was promoting *chaebols* that would have an international presence.

Even in the 1970s, as a consequence of the support of selected *chaebols* and badly formulated investments, the government was obliged to rescue many projects. The *chaebols*, through this policy, were encouraged to take excessive risks in the certain knowledge that the state would bail them out of difficulty or failed ventures. The *chaebols* were also encouraged to become involved in a wide range of industrial production. For instance, the larger conglomerates had up to 150 different product lines in numerous subsidiaries. Cross-subsidization of subsidiaries compounded the difficulty of identifying whether capital was being employed effectively or profitably. Many products were, indeed, being manufactured at a loss. Critically, the provision of policy loans was a form of financial repression that favoured a few companies but denied the loanable funds for the growth of small and medium-sized enterprises (SMEs), which had to rely on the 'curb market' for high cost loans. Thus, while this industrial strategy did provide the basis for spectacular expansion, it was not on a sound basis and relied upon government through the banking system bailing out possible industrial failures.

The effect of policy loans on the Korean economy were such that during the 1970s, on average, these loans were carrying negative real rates of interest, and the annual interest subsidy from the state grew from about three per cent of GNP to some ten per cent by the 1980s (Noland, 1996). Over this period, real rates of interest fell as policy loans increased. The burden of these policy loans fell on the Korean people, who received low or negative rates of interest on their savings. The policy of financial repression was to some degree a legacy of the Japanese colonial past. This was carried over into the post-civil war banking system in Korea and inhibited the growth of a properly functioning banking system. The policy of financial repression in Korea has resulted in the total amount of domestic savings in the economy being lower than they need have been; consumption among the people has been lower than it need have been; and investment resources have been allocated on the basis of non-economic criteria rather than on a rate of return basis.

The Park model did provide the single focus on industrialization and growth and proved a strength during the 1960s–70s, though as we have seen it was not without cost to the Korean people. The Park legacy has, however, left Korea with an industrial system that is too concentrated, relying on a few *chaebols* (Hyundai, Samsung, Daewoo, LG) with an international presence, and some 25 other *chaebols* dominating the economy. Critically, SMEs find it impossible to survive, let alone thrive, in such a financial system that is biased towards usually financing large conglomerates. The *chaebols'* and state influence on industrial policy has resulted in a misapplication of resources in the banking system and even to the *chaebols* themselves. The rate of return on investment projects for some *chaebols* is a mere one per cent and the banking system relies on providing negative returns to investors, or the state supporting their operations. Samsung, for example, had investment plans in 1995 that aimed to quadruple its sales by 2001 to US$200 billion. This would have been equivalent to the size of the entire industrial output of Sweden. Industrial policy in Korea encouraged the *chaebols* to take excessive risks and to develop grandiose plans that were breathtaking in their ambitions.

The Park legacy has resulted in an extreme form of moral hazard where the state cannot reconcile the need to open the economy to overseas investment, and, thus, provided the loanable funds for continuing economic growth and at the same time continued to interfere in the industrial policy of the economy. The future credibility of economic policy in Korea will depend upon a demonstration that growth can be maintained on the basis of a fully open economy where transparency and accountability for the use of investment resources is market determined and where the state withdraws from the interference in the economy. The two areas that need to be reformed are the banking sector and the ownership and financing of industrial organization. The introduction of equity capital instead of bank debt would provide a more sound and stable basis on which to develop industry. The crisis has indicated that internationally acceptable economic standards were not being met. Government support for projects in the industrial sector simply because of political connections and non-economic considerations is at the heart of the crisis and is not a basis for continuing economic growth.

CONCLUSION

The financial contagion in Asia has exposed an industrial policy that served Korea well in the past when the world economy was less open, but these same policies have now brought the economy to near-collapse. The future progress of the economy will be determined by the response of the Korean government to these changed circumstances by essentially causing it to withdraw from the process of formulating industrial policy and particularly to refrain from trying to promote strategy without regard to the economic and social costs of policy. Some 15 of the 30 *chaebols* are in receivership, or under government protection, and the banking system is similarly in crisis with over half the banks technically, if not actually, insolvent. Short term debt is estimated at between US$60–100 billion. The economic growth rate, which was projected at eight per cent, has been revised downwards to a more realistic two per cent. The international plans and investments overseas of the *chaebols* have been suspended as the economy faces retrenchment. Unemployment will at least double in the short run from the historically low two per cent. The IMF standby agreement is currently some US$37 billion as the minimum required support to stabilize the economy at a lower level of economic activity. The Koreans have reluctantly and, perhaps not convincingly, also agreed to some *chaebol* and bank closures or at least takeovers, while allowing foreign ownership to the extent of 51 per cent of equity in Korean companies. Short term debt is being rolled over to meet the repayment requirements of foreign creditors. The Won has also been floated to find its market value in the wake of the exhaustion of the central bank's foreign currency reserves.

Over the last 30 years Korea has made a number of major policy mistakes, as in the 1970s, but has also responded to exogenous shocks to the economy, rescuing economic growth and allowing prosperity to continue with their development model essentially intact. This current crisis, however, will require an order of change that is perhaps greater in testing Korean resolve to shift their industrial policy and reform their banking system in the full recognition that globalization is a force that no government or people can command. A more liberalized Korea would have weathered the financial problems in the region, and at a lower economic and social cost, than the present financial and economic structure will be able to do. Higher unemployment, social unrest and a fall in consumption, together with a loss of savings, will be the price that will be paid for economic policies that have outlived their usefulness. There is, however, one problem that could arise before the economy is fully stabilized and adjusted to the new banking and industrial policy that will emerge post-crisis – the collapse of the North Korean economy and society. If North Korea were to collapse in the near future, as opposed to in a few years' time, then Korea would be in a very weak position to cope with such a situation as well as its own economic problems.

NOTES

1. In this contribution, 'China' is used to refer to the People's Republic of China.
2. From now on, 'Korea' is used to refer to South Korea.

REFERENCES

Bae, J., Rowley, C., Kim, D.-H. and Lawler, J. (1997) 'Korean Industrial Relations at the Crossroads: The Recent Labour Troubles', *Asia Pacific Business Review*, Vol. 3, No. 3, pp. 148– 60.

Bergsten, F.C. (1997) 'The Asian Monetary Crisis: Proposed Remedies', *Institute For International Economics*, Washington DC, pp. 1–7.

Cathie, J. (1989) *Food Aid and Industrialisation: The South Korean Economy 1945–1986.* London: Avebury.

Chung, K.H., Lee, H.C. and Jung, K.H. (1997) *Korean Management: Global Strategies and Cultural Transformation.* Berlin: de Gruyter.

Das, D.K (1992) *Korean Economic Dynamism.* London: Macmillan.

Economist, The (1982) 'Determined to Win: A Survey of South Korea'.

Economist, The (1988) 'Stand Tall: A Survey of South Korea'.

Economist, The (1995) 'The House that Park Built: A Survey of South Korea'.

Fisher, S. (1998) *The Asian Crisis: A View from the IMF.* Washington DC, pp. 1–7.

International Monetary Fund (1997) 'IMF Approves SDR Stand-by Credit for South Korea', Press Release No.97/55, 4 December, pp. 1–4.

Kim J.-I. and Lau, L.J. (1994) 'The Sources of Economic Growth of the East Asian Newly Industrialized Countries', *Journal of the Japanese and International Economies*, No. 106, pp. 235–77.

Kuznets, P.W. (1977) *Economic Growth and Structure in the Republic of Korea.* US: Yale University Press.

Krugman, P. (1994) 'The Myth of Asia's Miracle', *Foreign Affairs*, Vol. 73, No. 6, pp. 62–78.

Liu, L., Noland, M., Robinson, S. and Wang, Z. (1998) 'Asian Competitive Devaluations', *Institute for International Economics*, Working Paper, 98-2, pp. 1–13.

Noland, M. (1996) 'Restructuring Korea's Financial Sector for Greater Competitiveness', *Institute for International Economics*, Apec Working Paper, 96-14, pp. 1–31.

Noland, M., Robinson, S. and Liu, L.-G .(1997) 'The Economics of Korean Unification', *Institute for International Economics*, Apec Working Paper, 97-5, pp. 1– 20.

Rodrik, D. (1994) 'King Kong Meets Godzilla: The World Bank and the East Asian Miracle', in A. Fishlow *et al.* (eds), *Miracle or Design? Lessons From the East Experience*. Washington DC: Overseas Development Council.

Rowley, C. (1997) 'HRM in the Asia Pacific Region: Convergence Questioned', *Asia Pacific Business Review*, Vol. 3, No. 4.

Sarel, M. (1996) 'Growth in East Asia: What We Can and What We Cannot Infer', *Economic Issues*, No. 1, International Monetary Fund ,Washington DC, pp. 1–14.

Solow, R.M. (1956) 'A Contribution to the Theory of Economic Growth', *Quarterly Journal of Economics*, No. 70, pp. 65–94.

Stewart, P. (1996) 'Japanese Management: The End of Modern Times?', *Asia Pacific Business Review*, Vol. 2, No. 4.

Wilkinson, B. (1994) *Labour and Industry in the Asia Pacific: Lessons from the Newly-Industrialized Countries*. Berlin: de Gruyter.

The Korean Electronics Industry:
The Japanese Role in its Growth

ROBERT J. CASTLEY

Several observers have noted that 'those countries which enjoyed the most rapid economic growth ... have highly dynamic electronic industries. This applied in particular to the four leading East Asian NIEs' (Kim, 1980). The electronics industry has become one of Korea's most important industries, and it accounted for an increasing share of output, exports and employment. Its spectacular growth can be largely attributed to its rapid export expansion (see Table 1). Since 1970, electronics has been one of Korea's top five exports. In 1988 it overtook textiles to become the dominant export, accounting for more than a quarter of total exports (see Table 2). This also made Korea the world's sixth largest exporter of electronic goods.

TABLE 1
GROWTH OF THE KOREAN ELECTRONICS INDUSTRY (US$ million)

	1967	1969	1971	1973	1975	1980
Production (a)	37	80	138	462	860	2,852
Exports (b)	7	42	89	369	582	2,004
(b) as % of (a)	18	52	64	79	68	70
Total exports (c)	320	623	1,068	3,221	4,885	17,214
(b) as % of (c)	2	7	8	10	12	12

Sources: Bank of Korea; Korea Fine Instruments Centre (KFIC).

TABLE 2
LEADING KOREAN EXPORTS (% share of total exports)

	1970	1975	1981	1985	1988
1st	Textiles (41)	Textiles (36)	Textiles (30)	Textiles (23)	Electronics (25)
2nd	Plywood (11)	Electronics (9)	Electronics (11)	Electronics (14)	Textiles (24)
5th	Electronics (4)				

Source: Compiled from Economic Planning Board data.

Despite this spectacular growth and export performance of electronics, few attempts have been made to determine the cause of its growth. It is widely held that its impressive growth rates, as with other industries, was mainly the result of the government's policy regime. Although it is

Robert J. Castley, Fellow of the University of Manchester.

generally believed that 'internal' factors were responsible for the rapid expansion of exports, there is intense debate over the relevant factors. The 'neoclassical school' (of economic development) attributes the rise of manufactured exports to the government's policy of establishing a suitable environment for the private sector, trade liberalization and investment in human resources. The 'statist school' attributes the success to direct government intervention in the form of incentives and subsidies, both direct and indirect. Kim (1980: 324) asserts that 'the government played a major role in the export expansion of the electronics industry'. Amsden (1989: 82) also stresses the role of the government its promotion. Given that the industry was highly export-orientated, one must treat with some suspicion the view that the state led in what was clearly an export led industry. The engine of growth was not the state, but exports.

ARGUMENTS, PERIODIZATION AND FRAMEWORK

However, the 'market' versus 'state' debate is only relevant if the contributing factors are internal, which both schools of development emphasize. Unfortunately, the 'external' factors that also contributed to the growth of industries in the newly industrializing economies (NIEs) have largely been ignored in the literature on East Asian development. The concentration on internal factors results in only a partial analysis, which inevitably distorts the overall picture. This article, therefore, adopts a different approach, for while it acknowledges the importance of internal factors (such as government incentives and creation of an export climate), it argues first, that the main stimulus to the growth of the industry came from external sources – in particular, Japanese firms and second, that domestic policies were only effective in so far as they were supported by external factors. The work concentrates on the formative years of the industry's growth (1967–76), partly because it is the 'start-up' period rather than the 'sustained growth' period (1977–81) that is of greater interest to developing countries seeking to emulate Korea's industrialization.

The electronics industry is usually subdivided into three subsectors: consumer electronics (radios, televisions [TVs]), industrial electronics (telecommunications), and electronic parts and components (semiconductors). The parts and components subsector dominated both output and exports. As early as 1968 it accounted for four-fifths of total electronics exports and half of total production. In the 1970s, parts and components exceeded the combined production of the other two subsectors and also accounted for 60 per cent of Korea's total electronics exports by 1975 (see Table 3). This analysis will, therefore, concentrate more on the parts and components subsector, which was crucial to the industry's development in the 1970s, the period in which the industry 'took-off'.

The framework used for the analysis here is the 'virtuous cycle'. As Shinohara (1982: 95) noted, successful Asian economics have experienced both 'export-orientated' and 'investment-orientated' types of growth:

TABLE 3
OUTPUT AND EXPORTS OF ELECTRONICS (US$ million)

	1968 Output	1968 Exports	%	1972 Output	1972 Exports	%
Consumer electronics	12.9	3.6	18	55.3	27.9	19
Industrial equipment	6.7	0.1	1	25.3	11.0	8
Parts and components	24.3	15.8	81	127.0	103.0	73
Total	45.9	19.5	100	207.6	142.1	100

	1975 Output	1975 Exports	%	1980 Output	1980 Exports	%
Consumer electronics	270.0	198.3	34	1,148	985	49
Industrial equipment	93.6	35.8	6	364	115	6
Parts and components	496.6	347.8	60	1,340	904	45
Total	860.3	581.9	100	2,852	2,004	100

because a virtuous-circular pattern of cumulative expansion has made its appearance between exports and investments; while the export-orientated type of growth has been tied in with the investment-orientated type, exports and investments provide mutual feedback. Should this export-orientated type stand alone be sustained, scepticism would arise about its continuity. Inevitably it would give rise to an investment boom at home, thereby reinforcing the competitive power of the export industries. A boom in investments would lead to a boom in exports, which in turn would naturally ignite another investment boom at home. If a domestic investment boom is generated in one country, there may be a sharp rise in its imports of capital good ... This constitutes a significant momentum in the process of feedback between export and investment; economic growth of this investment-orientated type cannot be assured unless there is a rise in the imports of capital goods.

Watanabe and Kajiwara (1983: 320) also note that the NIEs' economic growth was not based solely on an export-orientated industrialization drive, because:

These countries used their export earnings to import capital and intermediate goods and technologies, and this resultant capital formation further strengthened the international competitiveness of their manufactured exports, which in turn increased their capacity to invest. This mechanism of reciprocal inducement between export expansion and capital formation was the key to their success.

Consequently, the term 'export-orientated industrialization' needs to be redefined to include the operation of this cycle. The cycle between investment, imports competitiveness and exports is shown in Figure 1. Doubtless, there is much that governments can do to facilitate the operation of the cycle of manufactured exports. However, in the context of the Korean electronics industry, the main stimulus came, as this contribution will argue, from Japan.

FIGURE 1
INVESTMENT, IMPORTS, COMPETITIVENESS AND EXPORTS CYCLE

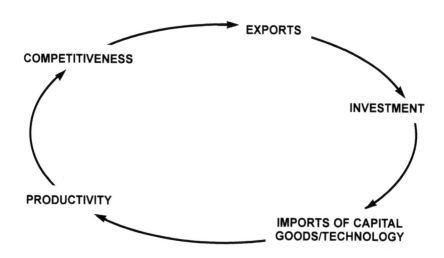

PATTERNS OF INVESTMENT

In the second Five Year Development Plan (1966–71), the Korean government expected the then electrical machinery sector to increase output. It was not until 1969 that the government promoted electronics as a strategic export industry through the Electronics Industry Promotion Law (modelled on the Japanese 1957 Act of Temporary Measures for Promotion of the Electronics Industry). The selection of electronics as a strategic industry was based on the following assumptions. First, that it would exploit Korea's comparative advantage in cheap labour for the labour intensive production processes (such as assembly). Second, that it would generate extensive employment. Third, that it would stimulate growth in other sectors of the economy through the purchase of local inputs (that is, through backward linkages). Fourth, that it would enable the transfer of foreign technology. Fifth, that there would be sufficient demand, particularly in overseas markets, where the popularity of electronics goods offered a strong growth potential. The 'Electronics Plan' covered the eight-year period

1969–76 and set a goal of US$ 400 million in exports – a target that was actually exceeded by over 150 per cent.

Nevertheless, the sudden growth of the industry and the existence of an extensive array of state incentives (such as long term loans, low interest rates, duty free imports and accelerated depreciation) is not evidence of the effectiveness of the state's role. The Korean government realized that it would have to depend on various forms of foreign investment and loans because the country lacked the expertise and funds to develop its own electronics industry. The investment surge that took place has to be seen in the context of what was happening in East Asia. Sony (which had introduced the transistor radio in 1955) sought cheap labour in offshore sites to undercut US and Japanese competitors. For example, it moved some production to Hong Kong in 1959. This move was soon followed by US electronic firms striving to maintain their competitive position. In the late 1960s, US firms (Motorola, Signetics, Fairchild and Control-Data) moved into Korea to combat Japanese success in penetrating US markets. However, the Japanese soon retaliated when Toshiba and Sony, followed by a host of others, including the largest such as Matsushita, Sanyo, Mitsubishi Electrical and NEC, entered Korea to produce a wide range of electronics, particularly parts and components (such as switches, resistors, condensers and transformers), to compete against US firms in international markets. The success of the earlier arrivals attracted more Japanese electronics firms, especially suppliers, so that by the mid-1970s, Japanese investment clearly exceeded that of the US. If loans are added, then the Japanese 'stake' in the industry was much higher (see Table 4). It would seem from this that the establishment of an electronics industry had more to do with Japanese–US competition than with Korean government policies.

TABLE 4
FOREIGN DIRECT INVESTMENT (FDI) AND LOANS IN THE ELECTRONICS INDUSTRY, 1975
(US$ million)

	US Loans	FDI	Japan Loans	FDI	Others Loans	FDI
Consumer and industrials	12.5	10.7	24.5	18.3	3.8	2.4
Parts and components	33.6	16.1	56.0	51.4	6.7	1.2

Source: Table 15.

However, the concern with overall amounts does not indicate the true impact of investment. A better guide are 'cases' – the actual number of investment projects and their spread by type of ownership. The Japanese dominated the number of cases throughout the 1970s and also spread their investments much more widely through joint ventures (JVs). The Japanese preferred JVs, unlike the Americans who preferred wholly owned subsidiaries. The Japanese share of all JVs in the electronics industry was 76 per cent; for parts and components it was as high as 91 per cent (see Table 5).

TABLE 5
FOREIGN OWNERSHIP OF PROJECTS AND OWNERSHIP (by number)

	Subsidiaries 1975[a]		JVs 1975[a]		Total cases 1980[b]	
	US	Japan	USA	Japan	US	Japan
Consumer and industrial	3	7	6	25	–	–
Parts and components	10	19	12	108	–	–
Total	13	26	18	133	32	153

Sources: [a] KFIC; [b] Ministry of Finance.

JAPANESE MOTIVES FOR INVESTMENT

The flow of investments into Korea's electronics industry cannot be attributed solely (or mainly) to Korea's investment incentives. Any assessment of the cause of foreign direct investment (FDI) must assess the effects of not only the 'host' country's policies but also the 'donor' country's policies. Given that the bulk of FDI in the 1970s was Japanese, it is necessary to examine the motives of Japanese investors, rather than the other investors. The reasons for the investments are very important because they determine the sales (of investing firms) by destination (exports) and the procurements by source (imports). The Japanese make a distinction between objective or aim (*mokuteki*) and motives (*doki*).

The late 1950s saw greatly increased production of household goods (such as refrigerators, tape recorders, electric saucepans and fans), followed by a boom in electronics (TVs, radios and transistors) in Japan. Two products in particular represent the growth of the Japanese electronics industry: the transistor boom from 1957 to 1962, and the production of integrated circuits (ICs) from 1962 onwards. The Japanese development of ICs is well known. At a very early stage (the mid-1960s), ICs were developed and applied to a wide range of products for mass markets (such as radios, TVs, tape recorders), as well as for industrial equipment (computers and telecommunications). Both transistors and ICs were developed by large Japanese companies (Sony, Mitsubishi, NEC and Matsushita). The Japanese transistor boom of the 1950s (for transistor radios) was replaced by the TV boom of the 1960s. By the mid-1960s the home market was nearing saturation point for many of these products (for example, black and white TVs) and subsequently the Japanese government encouraged manufacturers to export to the US and Europe. The very success of the Japanese in US markets forced American manufacturers to seek cheap offshore sites for assembly in order to compete. Then Japanese multinational companies (MNCs) similarly began to assemble overseas to reduce their labour costs in order to compete with US companies. Studies of Japanese affiliates in Asia (MITI, 1973) indicate that the main objective was to strengthen export, not domestic, markets, in Asia. In a survey of the motives of Japanese investors in Korea, the Economic Planning Board (1974) found that the main reasons for investment were low wages, higher profits and plant site. The domestic market motive only accounted for 21 per cent of the total. Since the low wage motive was to ensure competitiveness in international markets, we can assume that the dominant aim was to use Korea as an export platform.

'Push' Factors

The motivations can be divided into 'push' and 'pull' factors. On the push side, as we saw, the Japanese component manufacturers that had been supplying large US companies had been forced to shift their bases of operations to stay competitive in export markets as the latter began to look for cheaper sources of supply (Yoshiro, 1975). The second, often understated, factor, was the need to 'disguise' the source of origin in order to bypass trade restrictions and continue exporting to the US and European Community. The Japanese electronics companies were determined to tariff jump through FDI and technical cooperation into both the Korean and US markets. The third factor was the need to upgrade their production facilities. Thus:

> As far as Japan is concerned, Japanese producers and consumers are climbing the technological and quality ladder as fast as they can in a conscious effort to leave a safe distance between Japan and follower countries. For this reason, the Japanese have wittingly given up lower-order E and E products like conventional transistor radios, black and white TVs, ... complex sound systems, colour TVs, VTRs, computers, microelectronics, etc. (Dore, 1986)

By the mid-1960s, the Japanese were beginning to turn their attention to more upmarket products, such as colour TVs (CTVs) and computers, and hence to relocate the more labour intensive basic electronics (such as transistors) to offshore sites, particularly in Korea and Taiwan. Another reason was the need for Japanese firms to forge links with local firms, partly to prevent the latter from competing with Japan. The Japanese did not see their investment as resulting in serious job losses at home. As it was noted,

> In some developed countries, foreign direct investment by their companies is considered an equivalent of 'job exporters'. Japanese foreign direct investment increased rapidly during the 1970s and there was some fear of job exports at first. But it evaporated quickly. The dominant view today is that far from exporting jobs, Japanese companies have been using foreign direct investment as a means of creating jobs at home in Japan. This view is held not only by company management but also by trade unions and independent researchers. (ibid.)

A report released in 1981 concludes that FDI had positive effects on employment in Japan, and earlier misgivings about possible job exports were dissolved (ibid.). Indeed, production at the finishing stage in the host country requires imports of immediate inputs and capital goods from Japan. 'Thus, in so far as overseas production protects and promotes the markets for Japanese goods, foreign direct investment can be seen as a means of protecting and promoting Japanese employment in industries producing intermediate inputs and capital goods' (ibid.). Furthermore, workers made redundant by the relocation of CTV production in the US were more than absorbed in the expanding lines. The expansion of the industry in Korea was beneficial to Japan because additional output in the former 'induced' additional output in the latter: 'For instance a unit increase of final demand for electrical and electronic machinery ... in ROK had a co-efficient of 0.3715 ... in inducing the increase of total domestic output of intermediate goods in Japan' (Watanabe and Kajiwara, 1983: 321).

'Pull' Factors

The Japanese electronics MNCs (and suppliers) were independent and free to move to countries where labour and transport costs were low, and which gave them access to US markets. Electronics is an industry in which the production process can be divided into different operations. Thus, labour intensive stages, such assembly in consumer electronics and semiconductors, can be relocated. However, relocation is only profitable as long as transport costs do not outweigh the advantages of lower labour costs. Therefore, an important pull factor was geographical proximity, which reduced transport costs between suppliers and assemblers, between parent companies, subsidiaries and JVs, and subcontractors. Korea was an obvious choice, and one that was encouraged by the Japanese government for geo-economic and political reasons. The Japanese were instrumental in persuading the Koreans to establish the Mason free trade zone (which was sited on the coast facing Japan), in which the Japanese accounted for the overwhelming majority (90 per cent) of electronics firms, which were responsible for 62 per cent of the total free trade zone exports (Warr, 1984).

Quality was also a major Japanese concern. In a highly competitive industry, where much depended on marketing and brand images, the Japanese MNCs (which handled the trade) could not afford to allow their reputations to be dented by inferior production batches. Consequently, contracts to subcontractors were conditional on them meeting high standards. The close geographical proximity of Japan also enabled Japanese engineers and technicians to advise Korean firms on the required standards.

A favourable investment climate in Korea also helped, but since several other countries also offered attractive investment incentives without generating FDI, the government's role as a pull factor should not be exaggerated. The push factors appear to be the major determinants. In short, Korea was fortunate to be in the right place (geographical proximity) at the right time (the need for Japanese firms to find offshore sites).

FOREIGN DOMINATION OF THE INDUSTRY

Foreign firms dominated the electronics industry's output and exports at an early stage (see Table 6). Given the high proportion of Japanese investors by 1975, we can assume that the industry was largely Japanese dominated (see Table 7).

TABLE 6
FOREIGN SHARE OF ELECTRONIC OUTPUT AND EXPORTS (US$ million)

	Output Total	Exports Foreign investors' share	Total	Foreign investors' share
1969	79	42	42	77
1971	138	51	88	72
1973	463	51	369	69
1975	860	64	581	74
1978	2,271	54	1,359	61

Source: KFIC (1977).

TABLE 7
FOREIGN SHARE OF ELECTRONICS OUTPUT AND EXPORTS AND JAPANESE SHARE OF
FOREIGN FIRMS

1975	Output	Exports	Japanese Share of Foreign Firms	
			Firms	Capital
Foreign firms	37	51	56	58
JVs	27	23	87	88
Local firms	36	26	–	–

Source: KFIC.

By 1980, the degree of foreign domination in electronics declined, as more local firms, the *chaebols*, had emerged, particularly in consumer electronics. However, the hold foreign companies and JVs had in industrial and components subsectors was still strong, accounting for 62 per cent of the former's and 72 per cent of the latter's output (see Table 8). Bloom (1992) claims that Japanese firms were 'encouraged' to leave, but as Hobday (1994) notes, even as late as the 1980s Korean firms were still heavily dependent upon Japan (and the US) for key components, capital goods and materials for electronics. The Japanese had shifted their policy from JVs to original equipment manufacture (OEM) arrangements, which enabled them to benefit from the same advantages of FDI without the cost, namely procuring lower cost products and the flexibility of expanding capacity during surges in demand. All the leading *chaebols* (such as Samsung, Hyundai, Lucky-Goldstar and Daewoo), which had sizeable electronics affiliates, retained their ties with Japanese electronics MNCs. The larger Japanese firms preferred to enter into subcontracting or JVs with larger Korean firms, such as Samsung, which had their own (Korean) subcontractors (500 in the case of Samsung in 1977). Toshiba had a JV with Samsung (to produce VCRs), Sanyo with Samsung (to produce copiers) and Mitsubishi Electric with Goldstar Electronics (to produce electronics parts). The *chaebols* had to rely on the Japanese for parts and components (as well as capital and technology), since they lacked sufficient small subcontractors in Korea (Stevens, 1990).

TABLE 8
FOREIGN SHARE OF ELECTRONICS OUTPUT(%)

1980	Local	Joint	Foreign	Value (US$ million)
Consumer electronics	76	6	18	1,147
Industrial	38	54	8	364
Parts and components	28	38	34	1,340

Source: Yamauchi, cited in Stevens (1990: 155).

In the mid-1980s, the *chaebols* and Korean electronics companies undertook extensive OEM work for Japanese companies: Samsung (for Toshiba), Goldstar (for NEC and Matsushita), Daewoo (for NEC), Korea Trigem (for Seiko) and Anam industries (for Matsushita). It is estimated that for consumer electronics, OEM exports accounted for anywhere from 33 to 81 per cent of total exports in 1986 depending on the item, and the share of OEM sales was especially high, around 80 per cent (Ernst and O'Connor, 1992: 152). Korean firms, through assembly parts production and eventually OEM, gradually acquired the skills to produce quality products that could compete in international markets. In the late 1980s Korean firms learnt how to undertake their own marketing. In short, the 'initial growth' of the industry was stimulated by the Japanese, but the 'sustained growth' phase depended upon local firms working closely with Japanese companies. Hobday (1994: 345) provides an interesting example of how Samsung Electronics developed through a close association with Sanyo, Toshiba and NEC during its formative years. Although a 'dynamic entrepreneurial base is essential' (Hobday, 1995: 188), on its own it would not have succeeded, with or without government support.

IMPORT DEPENDENCE

In 1968, domestically produced parts and materials accounted for only eight per cent of the total; by 1972 this had only risen to 18 per cent. Although Korea had achieved high proportions of domestically produced parts for some products (for example, 90 per cent for radios, 85 per cent for telephone exchanges), in the major electronics products the proportion of foreign made components was very high. The main suppliers were Japan and the US. For instance, the Japanese supplied most electrical power machinery, switch gear, electrical machinery and telecom-munications equipment, whereas the US was the major suppliers of transistors (see Table 9).

TABLE 9
MAJOR ELECTRONICS IMPORTS

SITC*	Product	1970 (Jan.–June)		1971 (June–Dec.)		1973 (June–Dec.)	
		US$m	%	US$m	%	$m	%
72	Electricals	67	US 29	167	US 38	36	US 35
			Japan 36		Japan 38		Japan 46
722	Switch gear	28	Japan 29	51	Japan 35	52	Japan 67
724	Telecomms equipment	11	Japan 50	32	Japan 52	77	Japan 71
729	Electrical machinery, NES	23	Japan 56	68	US 59	215	USA 54
729.3	Transistors/valves	13	US 78	41	US 78	162	US 65

* Standard International Trade Classification

Source: Compiled from UN Commodity Tables.

Japanese affiliates tended to be highly dependent on imported inputs (from Japan). MITI studies of procurement practices of Japanese affiliates show that a large proportion of capital equipment and intermediate goods were purchased from Japan. Korean firms were also dependent upon Japanese suppliers. All three subsectors were heavily dependent upon Japanese parts and components. It is estimated that, overall, the electronics industry relied on Japan for 70 per cent of its component imports (Bello and Rosenfeld, 1990: 149). The dependence on imports was partly caused by the initial lack of Korean subcontractors, by Japan's interest in promoting her own exports of machinery and because, as Chung (1975: 16) put it, 'Some Korean businessmen, especially those of the older generation, turn to Japanese suppliers almost out of habit'. The Japanese electronics industry includes a host of small and medium-sized enterprises (SMEs) subcontracting to the large conglomerates. For example, in the parts and components sector, SMEs account for more than half of total employment in the industry, but only four per cent of total shipments (Otsuka, 1987). It is, therefore, reasonable to assume that the Japanese introduced the same practice in Korea, whereby Japanese firms would be largely responsible for exporting the produce of Korean SMEs. Local subcontracting firms were initially engaged in simple processing activities (such as assembly and production of basic parts), since their delivery dates and quality controls were not up to the standards expected by the Japanese for export markets. Consequently, the Japanese had to import more parts into Korea to compensate for the lack of suitable local content.

The Korean government tried to reduce this dependency on imported components by establishing set targets for 'localization'. However, it failed to achieve this aim. Even in the late 1980s, dependency ratios remained high. Bloom (1992: 61) noted that the reason for dependence on imported components 'was simply that no account had been made for changes in the product range. As products have been superseded by more advanced types, domestic parts production has been shown to be inadequate for the new products.' The Japanese, by being responsible for much of the industry's innovation, influenced the technology and the imports. Past Korean 'inadequacies' are only part of the story. Japanese investors were also keen to procure components from Japan, thereby stimulating the exports of Japanese capital and intermediate goods. As Watanabe and Kajiwara (1983: 322) noted, Korean industrialization benefited Japan through what they called this 'inducement effect'; that is, the expansion of their own exports.

The heavy dependence on imports from Japan was not offset by increases in electronics exports to Japan. Initially, the Japanese preferred a 'triangular trade pattern' (of processing Japanese imports in Korea for export to the US) to 'reverse imports' to Japan. Consequently, the trade deficit in electronics with Japan was partly offset by a surplus on trade with the US. In the mid-1970s, Japan increased imports of Korean electronics.

TECHNOLOGY IMPORTS

Although the Korean government encouraged domestic production, there was no local 'capability' so at a very early stage Korean entrepreneurs had to seek foreign assistance in the form of 'packaged technology' – that is, component parts, assembly processes, product specifications, technical personnel, production methods and quality controls (Kim, 1980). Even before the Normalization Treaty with Japan (1965), Sanyo and Matsushita (in 1962) had arranged assistance in the form of packaged technology with Goldstar for the production of radios, and also helped Goldstar to export radios to the US, thereby establishing indirect trade between Japan and the US.

The Koreans, lacking a self-sufficiently developed research and development (R&D) base, had little choice but to depend heavily on foreign technology, most of which was acquired from the Japanese (through FDI, JVs and licensing agreements). By 1974, Japan accounted for 84 per cent of the technology supplied to the Korean electronics industry. The industry's growth increased Korea's dependence on foreign technology, because to remain internationally competitive it could not rely on less than the latest production processes and product designs.

There was frequently a link between technology imports and imports of equipment and intermediate goods. Many of the technology import contracts included arrangements for the purchase (that is, imports) of Japanese parts and components (Chung, 1975). For example, Lucky-Goldstar had patent licensing agreements with Sony (VCRs), JVC (VCRs), Hitachi (VCRs, video compressors), Mitsubishi (microwave ovens), Toshiba (photocopiers), Matsushita (fax machines) and RCA (CTVs). Much of the imported technology was transferred more directly to JVs through assistance with production equipment, such as Lucky-Goldstar with several Japanese companies: Mitsubishi (electronic parts), Hitachi (machinery), NEC (telecommunications), Fuji (elevators) and Tanaka (metal products).

Since Korea was heavily dependent upon Japan for imports for the electronics industry, it follows that the former also imported the technology embodied in the imported capital equipment. The increase of investment in R&D in the 1980s did not noticeably reduce Korea's import dependence. As Bernard and Ravenhill (1995: 193) noted: 'ironically, the result of increased expenditure on R&D and the upgrading of production capabilities has been an increase in dependent patterns of procurement of components and capital goods'. Expanded exports enabled the industry to benefit from economies of scale, specialization, and new production methods and technologies. Export markets, as Kim (1980: 325) emphasized, 'became not only a source of stimuli for further development of the industry in terms of size and technology but also a source of stimuli for new product lines solely for overseas markets'. The extensive introduction of Japanese technology and production systems, plus training of technical personnel by Japanese affiliates (which were far more numerous than those of other investors), helped to raise the productivity and the competitiveness of Korean electronics. As Kim (1980) observed, 'the average annual production value per productive unit increased about four times from $5.8 million in 1970 to $22.4 million in 1975. Productivity per worker also increased . . . about 2.3 times from $3,600 to $8,340 in 1975.'

ELECTRONICS EXPORTS

The electronics industry's spectacular expansion in exports was largely due to foreign firms. As the Koreans officially recognized, 'This wonderful growth in production and exports was . . . contributed mainly by foreign investment firms' (Korean Development Bank, 1970). A study of foreign investment projects (883 in total) in 1974 found that the majority (760) of foreign firms were export-orientated (Jo, 1980: 141). JVs and foreign firms accounted for 79 per cent of exports in 1968, 71 per cent in 1972, and 74 per cent in 1975 (see Table 10). Since the vast majority of foreign firms and JVs were Japanese, we can safely conclude that the Japanese dominated the export sector. Korean firms (such as Goldstar, Tai Han Electric and Dong Nam Electric) mostly produced consumer electronics goods for the home market, but became more involved in exports on the basis of subcontracting for larger foreign (especially Japanese) companies (such as Samsung with Sanyo, and Goldstar with Alps Electronics).

Later, some Korean firms, as Bloom observed (1992: 114), became heavily dependent on OEM agreements linked to foreign component supplies, and 'This was in fact inevitable ... with limited technology base, negligible brand recognition overseas and no international marketing presence, there were few alternatives for an industry ... where technology – and thereby products – is continually changing.'

TABLE 10
ELECTRONICS EXPORTS BY INVESTOR (US$ million, rounded)

	Total	Local	JV	Foreign
1968	20	4	2	14
1970	55	15	8	33
1972	142	41	24	78
1973	369	115	73	181
1975	581	151	135	296

Source: EIAK.

The US was the major export destination for much of the electronics sector. In 1969, the US accounted for 77 per cent, and Japan only 3 per cent, of electronics exports. However, by 1974 Japan's share had grown to 25 per cent. During a critical stage of the development of the industry, the combined US and Japanese markets accounted for 89 per cent of all electronics exports. Although the North American and Japanese markets slowly declined (not in absolute terms, but in share of total exports) during the 1970s, they still accounted for two-thirds of Korea's exports in electronics (see Table 11).

TABLE 11
DESTINATION OF ELECTRONICS EXPORTS (US$ million)

	1974		1977		1979	
	Amount	% rounded	Amount	% rounded	Amount	% rounded
North America	332.6	64	541.9	53	865.1	47
Japan	128.2	25	177.7	17	237.4	17
Others	57.0	11	311.0	30[a]	664.3	36
Total	518.5	100	1,036.7	100	1,845.4	100

[a]Mainly Hong Kong (7%) and West Germany (7%).

Source: EIAK.

The major export in the early 1970s was transistors (and valves), which (in 1973) accounted for 62 per cent of total exports of electrical machinery (see Table 12). Most transistors (79 per cent) were exported to North America. US firms tended to concentrate on semiconductors and ICs mainly for export back to the US market, whereas Japanese firms concentrated more on transistors, as well as semiconductors and consumer electronics, also for the US market. This partly reflected the different approaches adopted by US and Japanese firms; the former tended to gear up for parts production for mainframe computers, whereas the latter concentrated on faster growing markets, namely electronics parts for consumer goods.

Both American and Japanese firms exported to the US. However, given the predominance of Japanese investments in the electronics industry, and the tendency of those Japanese firms that had invested in Korea to bring their US customers with them, it is reasonable to assume that Japanese affiliates contributed more to the export of electronics to the US, thereby creating a triangular pattern of trade. In US markets, the Japanese steadily relinquished their niche in the lower end to the NIEs (see Table 13), which moved into the markets previously opened up by the Japanese.

TABLE 12
ELECTRONICS EXPORTS BY PRODUCT (US$ million)

| SITC | Product | Exports, Jan.–June 1973 | | |
		Total	Japan	US
72	Electrical machinery	120.9	21.0	68.0
722.1	Electrical power machinery	4.2	3.1	0.1
722.2	Switch gear	4.2	2.8	0.2
724	Telecommunication equipment	26.3	3.0	16.5
724.1	TVs	6.8	0.5	6.1
724.2	Radios	11.5	1.6	6.1
729	Electrical machinery NES	85.1	11.3	50.0
729.3	Transistors, valves	75.0	7.5	48.1

Source: UN Commodity tables.

TABLE 13
ASIAN SHARES OF US MARKET (%)

Product		Japan	Korea	Hong Kong	Singapore
TVs	1969	85	–	0.5	–
	1973	51	3	–	–
	1977	61	7	–	–
Radios	1969	68	1	13	–
	1973	56	3	17	4
	1977	47	7	16	4
Electronics parts	1969	19	9	16	4
	1973	7	12	11	22
	1977	10	15	6	18

Source: UN World Trade Annual Statistics cited in Yamazawa and Watanabe (1988).

TABLE 14
ELECTRONICS AND ELECTRICAL GOODS:
JAPANESE AND KOREA EXPORTS (as % of world trade exports)

Product	Japan	Korea	Total world exports, 1979 (US$ billion)
Telecommunications	27	3	25
Domestic electrical appliances	11	0.4	7
Electrical machinery NES	12	2	33
Watches	21	2	6
Toys	9	5	6
Sound recorders	63	4	4

Source: Adapted from Turner and McMullen (1982: Table 4.1).

After 1970, the import share of the NIEs in the Japanese market for labour intensive goods rose rapidly. Factors affecting the penetration of Japanese markets included tariff reductions, abolition of import quotas and the use of Japanese intermediaries (often the 'parent' firm) to circumvent the complicated distribution networks in Japan, and in particular the tendency for Japanese firms to upgrade their own products, which created a niche for cheaper (albeit lower quality) imports. Of Japan's total imports of radios and TVs in 1979, Korea supplied 16 per cent, and Taiwan 23 per cent (Yamazawa *et al.*, 1983). Relocation to Korea was not a serious threat to Japan's slice of international trade in electronics and electrical goods, as Table 14 clearly shows. There was a degree of complementarity. In 1975, whereas the Koreans exported mostly parts and components (which accounted for 60 per cent of total electronics exports), the Japanese in contrast exported mostly finished products (which accounted for 76 per cent of their total electronics exports).

CONCLUSION

Electronics in Korea became an increasingly important industry during the 1970s, primarily because of its impressive export performance. The industry was dominated by foreign (mainly Japanese) investors. Although the government had actively intervened to attract foreign investment and create a competitive environment, it would seem that the more important determinant was the restructuring of the Japanese electronics industry (which subsequently affected Japan's overseas investment and trade policies). The relative importance of foreign investment in manufactured exports is usually difficult to explain. However, by concentrating on a major export industry, it is possible to establish a causal link between Japanese investments and the expansion of trade (both exports and imports). Because the composition of exports determined the growth and structure of the industry, and because Japanese firms were largely responsible for exports, then it follows that the Japanese were primarily responsible for the shaping of the Korean electronics industry in the 1970s. The key growth subsector was parts and components, which during the first half of the 1970s accounted for nearly two-thirds of output and more than three-quarters of exports. This sector was the main target of Japanese investments, accounting for a majority of the firms, 127 out of 151 in 1975, and the amount invested, US$ 51 million out of a total of US$ 69 million (see Table 15).

The consumer electronics subsector, which grew rapidly during the 1970s, also received considerable support from Japanese JVs. On the supply side, the Japanese were influential in terms of investments, loans, skill training, imports of capital and intermediate goods and technology transfers. On the demand side, it appears that Japanese firms and JVs, through their overseas marketing networks and subcontractual arrangements, expanded Korean exports of electronics to the US and other

TABLE 15
FOREIGN INVESTMENT IN ELECTRONICS BY TYPE AND NATIONALITY
US$ '000)

December 1975	Subsidiaries		Joint venture		Total Case	Total	
	Case	Amount	Case	Amount		Amount	Composition ratio (%)
USA	13	22,865 (39,264)*	18	4,003 (6,892)	31	26,868 (46,156)	26.8 (24.5)
Consumer and industrial equipment	3	9,621 (11,121)	6	1,083 (1,413)	9	10,684 (12,534)	10.7 (9.1)
Parts and components	10	13,244 (28,143)	12	2,940 (5,479)	22	16,184 (33,622)	16.1 (24.5)
Japan	26	34,032 (39,232)	133	35,729 (45,175)	159	69,761 (80,407)	69.6 (58.7)
Consumer and industrial equipment	7	10,295 (11,495)	25	8,029 (12,954)	32	18,324 (24,449)	18.3 (17.8)
Parts and components	19	22,737 (23,737)	108	27,700 (32,221)	127	51,437 (55,958)	51.3 (40.8)
Others	4	2,155 (7,655)	2	1,490 (2,856)	6	3,645 (10,511)	3.6 (7.7)
Consumer and industrial equipment	2	955 (955)	2	1,490 (2,856)	4	2,445 (3,811)	2.4 (2.8)
Parts and components	2	1,200 (6,700)	-	-	2	1,200 (6,700)	1.2 (4.9)
Total	43	59,052 (82,151)	153	41,222 (54,923)	196	100,274 (137,074)	100.00 (100.0)
Consumer and industrial equipment	12	20,871 (23,571)	33	10,582 (17,223)	45	31,453 (40,794)	31.4 (29.8)
Parts and components	43	38,181 (58,580)	120	30,640 (37,700)	151	68,821 (96,280)	68.6 (70.2)

* Figures in parentheses involve foreign loans.

Source: KFIC.

third country markets. The Japanese were also responsible for the expansion of electronics goods in the domestic Japanese market, which throughout the 1970s remained the second most important market (after the US). In short, the Japanese were largely responsible for the development of the 'virtuous circle'. Like the sixteenth century merchant in Europe, Japanese firms 'put out' (via FDI and subcontracting) labour intensive processes (assembly and parts production) in a complex production system. It was only towards the end of the 1970s that Korean *chaebols* emerged as major producers and exporters of electronics. Nevertheless, the industry remained closely tied to Japan through a complex network of suppliers and buyers. Local producers had to serve a long apprenticeship before they could master all the stages in production systems. Government policies also helped to facilitate growth. However, the engine of growth was neither the government nor local entrepreneurs, but foreign interests, motivated by global rather than local (that is, Korean) considerations. Local entrepreneurs only managed to expand production and exports as a result of extensive JV and subcontractual ties with Japanese firms. The US had introduced assembly work in the late 1960s, but it was the Japanese (through subcontracting of parts and components) that enabled the industry to achieve OEM production status.

Overall, it is reasonable to conclude that the export growth of the Korean electronics industry was largely due to the stimulus provided by Japanese investment and external marketing networks, which in turn were determined primarily by 'home' country factors rather than 'host' country incentives. Hence, the growth of Korean electronics was not so much a national, but instead a regional, phenomenon, partly based on a triangular trade pattern that was largely masterminded by the Japanese. Consequently, the growth of the industry can only be understood in the context of regional factors. To discuss the development of the industry without a knowledge of what was happening elsewhere (in this case the restructuring of Japanese electronics) is to compound the confusion surrounding the causes of its spectacular growth. On the other hand, by establishing linkages to the Japanese economy we are able to more clearly determine the reasons for the remarkable export expansion of electronics which contributed to the rapid growth of the industry. The domination of foreign (mainly Japanese) firms in the growth of the electronics industry in the 1970s undermines the claims of both schools of development economics on trade expansion, as they attribute growth to internal factors (that is, neutral trade regimes versus state intervention policies) and neglect external factors. There was a convergence of interests between Koreans who wanted access to technology and markets, and the Japanese, who sought low cost labour and sites. Without the assistance of foreigners in penetrating overseas markets, Korean electronics would not have become a successful export-led industry.

The implication of Korea's experience for other developing countries is that governments cannot adopt a 'do-it-yourself' approach to the development of such a complex industry. Internal factors, such as government support, were by themselves insufficient. Domestic policies did not have an independent effect. Without external support there would seem to be little prospect of emulating Korea's success in developing an industry that became an important part of its export-led industrialization drive. It is interesting to observe the 'dependence' of Thailand, Malaysia and the Philippines (which have developed electronics industries) on Japan and the NIEs, which now provide external support (Ernst and O'Connor, 1992).

NOTE

1. In this contribution 'Korea' is used to refer to South Korea.

REFERENCES

Amsden, A.H. (1989) *Asia's Next Giant: South Korea and Late Industrialization*. Oxford: Oxford University Press.
Bello, W. and Rosenfeld, S. (1990) *Dragons in Distress: Asia's Miracle Economies in Crisis*. San Francisco, CA: Institute for Food and Development Policy.
Bernard, M. and Ravenhill, J. (1995) 'Beyond Product Cycles and Flying Geese', *World Politics*, 47, January.
Bloom, M. (1992) *Technological Change in the Korean Electronics Industry*. Paris: OECD.
Chung, Mo (1975) 'Commercial Transfer of Foreign Technology', *Asian Economics*, No. 13, December.
Dore, R. (1986) *Structural Adjustment in Japan 1970–82*. Geneva: ILO.
Economic Planning Board (1979) *Foreign Direct Investment Special Survey*. Seoul.
Economic Planning Board (various dates) Manufacturing and Mining Surveys.
Ernst, D. and O'Connor, D. (1992) *Competing in the Electronics Industry*. Paris: OECD.
Hobday, M. (1994) 'Export-led Technology Development', *Development and Change*, Vol. 25.
Hobday, M. (1995) 'East Asian Latecomer Firms: Learning the Technology of Electronics', *World Development*, Vol. 23, No. 7.
Ichimera, S.I. (ed.), *Challenge of Asian Developing Countries*. Tokyo: Asian Productivity Organization.
Jo, S.-H. (1980) 'Direct Foreign Investment', in G.K. Park (ed.), *Macroeconomics and Industrial Development in Korea*. Seoul: KDI.
Kim, L.L. (1980) 'Stages of Development of Industrial Technology', in G.K. Park. (ed.), *Macroeconomics and Industrial Development in Korea*. Seoul: KDI.
Koo, B.Y. (1985) 'Direct Foreign Investment in Korea', in W. Galenson (ed.), *Foreign Trade and Investment*. Madison, WI: University of Wisconsin Press.
Korean Development Bank (1970) *Industry in Korea*. Seoul.
MITI (1973) *Survey of Investors in NICs*. Tokyo: Industrial Policy Bureau.
Otsuka, S. (1987) 'Korean Parts and Components Suppliers', in I. Sakong (ed.), *Macroeconomic Policy and Industrial Development Issues*. Seoul: KDI.
Shinohara, M. (1982) *Industrial Growth, Trade and Dynamic Patterns in the Japanese Economy*. Tokyo: University of Tokyo Press.
Stevens, R. (1990) *Japan's New Imperialism*. London: Macmillan.
Turner, L. and McMullen, N. (eds) (1982) *The Newly Industrialising Countries' Trade and Adjustment*. London: Unwin.
Warr, P.G. (1984) 'Mason Free Trade Zone: Benefits and Costs', *The Developing Economies*, Vol. 22, No. 2.
Watanabe, T. and Kajiwara (1983) 'Pacific Manufactured Trade and Japan's Options', *Developing Economies*, Vol. 21, No. 4, December.
Yoshiro, M.Y. (1975) 'Japanese Foreign Direct Investment', in Frank (ed.), *The Japanese Economy: International Perspectives*. Washington, DC: Johns Hopkins University Press.
Yamazawa, I. and Watanaba T. (1988) 'Industrial Restructuring and Technology Transfer', in
Yamazawa I., Taniguchi, K. and Hirata, A. (1983) 'Trade and Industrial Adjustment in PacificAsian Countries', *Developing Economies*, Vol. 21, No. 4.

Latecomer Catch-up Strategies in Electronics: Samsung of Korea and ACER of Taiwan

MIKE HOBDAY

The newly industrializing economies (NIEs) of East Asia, most notably the Republic of Korea[1] and Taiwan, have become formidable international competitors in electronics. Exports of electronics have played a major part in both countries' economic progress since the 1960s while, during the 1980s and 1990s, further rapid growth and a technological upgrading of production occurred. Although the general economic achievements of the NIEs are well documented, far less is known about the strategies by which East Asian firms acquired foreign technology, learned to innovate and managed to catch up in electronics.[2]

The purpose of this contribution is to examine the cases of Samsung Electronics Co. (SEC) of Korea and ACER of Taiwan to generate insights into how firms managed to overcome barriers to entry in electronics and become strong competitors on the world stage. Both firms are leading national exporters of electronics and both have provided role models for other aspiring East Asian companies to follow. SEC is an example of a large conglomerate successfully diversifying into electronics, while ACER began more recently as a small Taiwanese start-up company.[3]

Compared with Japan, Taiwan and Korea are genuine 'latecomer' economies, having little industrial history prior to the 1950s. Therefore, the notion of the latecomer firm to describe the particular conditions facing East Asian developing country competitors in electronics starts our analysis. This idea contrasts with the conventional notion of innovation 'leaders' and 'followers' in advanced country markets. Next we briefly discuss the historical and international contexts, illustrating both countries' remarkable performance in electronics exports. The mechanisms by which local companies acquired foreign technology are also touched upon. Following on, we look at the cases of SEC and ACER in turn to show how these particular latecomer firms learned process and product technologies.[4] We highlight the sources, paths and patterns of learning in the firms, relating these patterns to corporate strategy, company organization, innovation and performance. The next section interprets the evidence by proposing a simple model of how latecomer firms progressed up the technological ladder within the original equipment manufacture (OEM) system.[5] The model applies not only to SEC and ACER, but also to other latecomer firms such

Mike Hobday, Science Policy Research Unit, University of Sussex as Lucky Goldstar, Daewoo and Hyundai from Korea and Tatung and Mitac of Taiwan. We then counterpoise the empirical findings with traditional models of innovation and modern resource-based theories of the firm, pointing to the need for further theoretical work to properly understand the processes and paths of East Asian latecomer innovation. The conclusion draws attention to strengths, weaknesses, challenges and prospects facing latecomer firms as the year 2000 approaches.

Although an analysis of government's role in encouraging competitiveness is outside our scope, it is important to stress that substantial policy differences exist between East Asian countries, as do unresolved debates over the patterns and consequences of government intervention (Amsden, 1989; Wade, 1990; World Bank, 1993). Nevertheless, most observers agree that East Asia's latecomer firms flourished, until recently, within conditions of macroeconomic stability, high rates of saving and low inflation. Also important were outward looking, export-led industrial policies and governments' commitment to education, especially vocational training, across the region. In some cases (such as Korea), government also intervened directly to ensure the entrepreneurial base was sufficiently strong to lead industrialization. While debates over the merits and outcomes of direct industrial intervention continue, there can be little doubt that without the tenacity, capabilities and creative strategies of latecomer firms, policies could not have succeeded and progress in electronics would not have occurred in the remarkable manner witnessed.[6]

THE IDEA OF THE LATECOMER FIRM

Most modern, dynamic theories of the firm assume that companies have access to technological resources and competencies through their interaction with the environment in which they compete. Building on the original resource-based work of Penrose (1959), authors such as Teece *et al.* (1994) and Dosi (1988) have proposed a 'dynamic capabilities' view of the firm. Others have sought to provide dynamic models of innovation to deepen our understanding of firm processes, stages of development and strategic opportunities arising from core competencies (Utterback and Abernathy, 1975; Abernathy *et al.*, 1983; Hamel and Prahalad, 1994; Chesbrough and Teece, 1996; Tushman and O'Reilly, 1997). Usually, the theoretical discussion assumes a developed country context, with surrounding technological resources to draw upon and demanding markets to guide firms' decisions and influence their visions of the future (Ansoff and Stewart, 1967; Swann and Gill, 1993). However, in developing (or latecomer) economies, this dynamic 'Schumpeterian' environment cannot be assumed. Firms often operate within small, underdeveloped markets, and the educational and skills infrastructure is usually sadly lacking. Indeed, these were precisely the conditions facing Korea and Taiwan when they embarked upon industrialization in the 1950s and 1960s.[7]

To help understand the innovation paths, achievements and problems facing firms which have emerged as international competitors from the NIEs, the idea of the latecomer firm can be helpful.[8] In contrast to a leader or follower, a latecomer firm is an industrial enterprise (existing or potential) that confronts at least two major barriers to entry in attempting to compete in advanced (usually export) markets: (a) technological disadvantages; and (b) market disadvantages.[9] Technological barriers exist because the firm is located in a developing country and it is, to a large extent, dislocated from the main international sources of innovation and research and development (R&D). The latecomer competes in isolation from the world centres of science and technology and, typically, will lag behind in engineering competence, technical skills and R&D capabilities. Unlike the leader or follower, the latecomer's surrounding industrial and technological infrastructure will be poorly developed. Universities may be inadequately financed and other educational and technical institutions poorly equipped. According to most conventional wisdom, access to technological competencies and a healthy surrounding 'national system of innovation' are important for corporate competitiveness (Nelson and Rosenberg, 1993). Therefore, to succeed in international export markets, the latecomer firm must devise and implement a strategy to overcome these technological disadvantages. In the cases of Korea and Taiwan these disadvantages were particularly acute in the 1950s and 1960s, as noted earlier.

Markets and marketing represent the second latecomer disadvantage. In addition to its technological problems, a latecomer firm will typically be dislocated from the fast growing, advanced international markets it needs to supply in order to succeed. These markets tend to be located in the advanced countries where consumer tastes have developed alongside sophisticated marketing and distribution channels. The latecomer firm, in contrast to the leader and follower, will normally face underdeveloped, often small, local markets, unsophisticated users and poor domestic market growth prospects. Again, according to received wisdom, user–producer linkages and industrial clusters of leading edge suppliers and producers are a vital part of company innovation and competitive performance, as well as wider industrial development.[10] Therefore, to reach the status of a strong international competitor, latecomers such as SEC and ACER had to devise strategies to overcome market barriers to entry, build robust channels into overseas markets and then forge the user–producer linkages that stimulate technological advance. This poses extreme difficulties for most latecomer firms located, as they are, in developing countries. In short, the latecomer has to develop its marketing skills and competencies outside the major international clusters of innovative suppliers and users.

Latecomers can be treated as a distinct analytical category, different from leaders and followers. A technology leader (for example, Intel or IBM) will have the competence to develop new products and processes to give it important advantages in the marketplace. A leader, typically, will enjoy the benefits of an effective R&D department capable of generating product innovations, novel processes and, perhaps, important new materials. By these means the leader contributes to and, sometimes, advances the world technology frontier. In contrast to a latecomer, a leader will often benefit from strong and useful connections with universities.

Latecomer firms are also distinct from technology followers[11] who, like leaders, are linked into advanced markets and often have access to leading edge technology. In some cases, agile followers have advantages over leaders. Due to their competencies, followers may be able to learn rapidly from the experience of leaders, avoid R&D costs through imitation, and quickly improve upon a product, or align it more closely to a buyer's need.[12] Fairchild, for example, was the leader in the eight bit microprocessor but soon lost its initial lead to followers Zilog, Intel and Motorola. These companies improved upon the basic Fairchild design and gained follower advantages (Langlois *et al.*, 1988: 15).

Although the advantages of leaders and followers cannot be exploited by latecomers, the latter generally have substantial labour cost advantages and this can form one part of their initial entry strategy. However, to catch up with firms in advanced countries, latecomers have to devise and implement strategies that enable them not only to overcome initial entry barriers, but also to continuously and systematically build up their competencies, skills and resources. Just how large, successful latecomer firms such as SEC and ACER overcame these daunting disadvantages and forged inroads into advanced markets is largely unexplored in the economic and management literature on firms. Yet, these companies are remarkable examples of rapid latecomer catch-up growth, learning and innovation. However, before examining them it is useful to place them in their historical context of technological development and the general advance of latecomer electronics firms from Korea and Taiwan.[13]

ELECTRONICS IN KOREAN AND TAIWAN

Industrial and Technological Progress

Both Korea and Taiwan have made considerable progress in electronics since the 1960s and especially during the 1980s and 1990s. Electronics exports from Korea grew from just US$ 2 billion in 1980 to US$ 20 billion in 1991, overtaking textiles and garments, steel, shipping and automobiles to become the largest single export sector. Taiwan, with a much smaller population, exported around US$ 12.2 billion in electronics in 1991.[14] Further rapid growth occurred in the early 1990s, by which time many latecomers were able to design their own products and the technological gap between themselves and market leaders had narrowed considerably. Some, such as SEC, had overtaken market leaders in key areas such as dynamic random access memory (DRAM) semiconductors.

Korea's electronics industry began with the production of valve (vacuum tube) radios in the late 1950s. Several American transnational corporations (TNCs) set up wholly owned subsidiaries in the mid-1960s to assemble semiconductors (or chips) using cheap local labour, though according to Bloom (1991: 8–10) they imparted little technological know-how. By contrast, Japanese firms formed joint ventures (JVs) and often provided technical assistance to local companies. Matsushita and Sanyo supplied technology to Samsung and Goldstar during 1961 and 1962 to help them set up transistor radio factories. Toshiba set up a JV and began two major technical agreements with local electronics firms in the late 1960s. Japanese companies used JV much more extensively than US firms, both to gain entry into local markets and to use East Asian companies as contract manufacturers. US firms, by contrast, saw Korea as a direct investment centre for low cost exports.

Similarly, Taiwan's electronics industry began with the assembly of transistor radios in the late 1950s and black and white televisions (TVs) and semiconductor assembly in the early 1960s. In 1963 Sanyo formed a JV with a Taiwanese importer, starting up the first local production of air conditioners and audio electronics. Philips (of the Netherlands) began assembling resistors and capacitors in the Kaosiung free trade zone in 1966 and in 1970 began making black and white TVs. RCA started producing memory circuits in 1969 and black and white TVs and monitors for re-export back to the US in 1971. Many other foreign investors entered Taiwan included Sanyo, Matsushita, Orion, Sony, Sharp and Hitachi from Japan, and General Instruments and Texas Instruments (TI) from the US. Many local firms rushed in to provide subcontracting services to the TNCs.

During the electronics start-up phase in both countries, foreign companies acted as examples for local firms. They helped initiate the first electronics ventures and started up the export industries. They also began training local engineers and technicians, transferring valuable foreign technical and management skills.

During the 1970s, exports of simple manufactured goods and components grew rapidly as latecomers learned to manufacture many of the new products generated in the West and Japan. Often, local firms began as assemblers of simple products, buying the necessary inputs from the growing number of specialist parts suppliers. At the same time, large numbers of foreign buyers entered East Asian markets to source low cost consumer goods. New product lines included colour televisions (CTVs), digital watches, calculators, push-button telephones and TV video games. Some local firms mastered the production technology for these goods, though many relied on buyers for technical assistance.

In Korea, Sanyo, NEC and other large Japanese TNCs set up wholly owned subsidiaries, and by 1976 around 50 per cent of electronics output was produced in foreign or jointly owned factories (Bloom, 1991: 10). During the 1970s, the Korean conglomerates (or *chaebol*) strengthened their connections with Japanese electronics producers. SEC and Goldstar gained technology mainly through licensing and subcontracting arrangements with Japanese firms. The latecomers also began rudimentary R&D to reverse engineer products and to learn how to improve processes.

In Taiwan, during the mid-1970s Philips began making CTVs in Kaosiung, while RCA transferred metal oxide semiconductor (MOS) technology to firms through the government's Industrial Technology Research Institute (ITRI). IBM and other large American TNCs began buying large quantities of computer subassemblies from local firms, leading to the start up of the computer industry in Taiwan. Later in the 1970s, ACER and others began producing at more advanced technology levels. However, most were very small and depended heavily on the TNCs' subcontract orders.

During the 1980s, exports of electronics exploded in both countries and the industry diversified into professional electronics, computers, peripherals, telephone handsets, key systems, and many other goods. Latecomer firms continued to build up their production expertise, and in the latter half of the 1980s began large scale exports of high quality precision engineered goods such as hard disk drives, colour display terminals, personal computers (PCs), video graphic adapters, camcorders, cameras, colour terminals and semiconductors.

In both Taiwan and Korea, local firms gained larger shares of production and began to introduce their own designs for low end (that is, lower price, less complex) goods. In Korea, employment in foreign subsidiaries fell by one-third between 1976 and 1985, despite the 50 per cent growth in electronics employment. With the rise of Korean firms, Japanese TNCs withdrew. Earlier, in 1980, Matsushita had pulled out of its JV with Anam Electric. Sanyo withdrew from its JV with SEC in 1983, NEC withdrew from its JV with Goldstar Electric in 1987. According to Bloom (1991: 9), Japanese firms left because of Korean government policies, including the withdrawal of the special tax benefits for investors.

In Taiwan, the production value of computing and related goods overtook consumer goods in the 1980s. IBM, Wang and Hitachi purchased very large quantities of computers and peripherals from local companies. By the late 1980s, wages had risen and Taiwan's main cost advantage had progressed from labour to high quality engineering. TNCs and other foreign buyers further increased their purchasing of keyboards, computer mice, TV monitors, printed circuit boards and printers.

During the 1980s, Korea became a major supplier of DRAMs, while in Taiwan at least five companies began fabricating semiconductors. Philips began a JV with the Taiwanese government in 1987 to form the Taiwanese Semiconductor Manufacturing Corporation to make specialist circuits for local design firms. In 1991, TI and ACER formed a partnership to produce memory circuits.

During the 1990s, the latecomer firms exported more sophisticated electronics, requiring complex software skills, advanced manufacturing know-how and semiconductor design capabilities. In order to overcome their dependency on OEM, some firms increased their marketing and R&D spending. Nevertheless, while the larger latecomers such as SEC narrowed the gap, most remained well behind the technology frontier set by the international leaders.

Despite their advances, most of the R&D efforts of Korean and Taiwanese firms remain applied, near-market developments, targeted at improving products and manufacturing processes. To date, there has been little investment in products new to the world or for extending the boundaries of R&D in the basic fields of electronics. Most latecomers still depend on Japanese and US suppliers for technology inputs, capital goods, core designs and key components. Much of Korea's production is in low end goods and, while the engineering base of many firms is strong, most firms have yet to establish the R&D, software and design strengths to enable them to compete with leaders at the technology frontier.

International Sources of Technology

Latecomer learning has depended on a variety of international channels of technology. Usually, foreign firms supply technology in return for a payment or a service, such as low cost production. The main channels, shown in Table 1, evolved through time as latecomers developed and sought to acquire more complex technologies.[15] In order to acquire foreign technology, local firms had to invest in their own training, skills, R&D and other competence building, not only for technology, but also in related areas such as finance, management and marketing.

TABLE 1
MECHANISMS OF FOREIGN TECHNOLOGY ACQUISITION IN ELECTRONICS

Mechanism

Foreign direct investment
Joint ventures
Licensing
Original equipment manufacture
Original design and manufacture
Subcontracting
Buyers and traders (foreign and local)
Informal means (copying, overseas training, hiring, returnees)
Overseas acquisitions/equity investments
Strategic partnerships for technology

Source: see text.

These channels enabled latecomers to acquire technology and enter export markets in various ways. Foreign direct investment (FDI) and JVs were important starting points for electronics, sparking off new export lines. Some foreign firms were imitated by local companies. Others assisted local firms with training under subcontracting and licensing agreements. Many TNCs hired and trained local technicians and supervisors in their subsidiaries. Major groups, such as Tatung of Taiwan, acquired training and engineering support in JVs. Under licensing deals, local firms paid for the right to manufacture products, sometimes for the local market. The TNCs would then transfer the necessary technology, particularly for low end goods which they were attempting to exit. Usually, licensing required more competence than a JV (in the latter the senior partner would often train the local company). In Taiwan, between 1952 and 1988 the government approved more than 3,000 licensing agreements (mostly in electronics), often including formal technology transfer clauses (Dahlman and Sananikone, 1990: 78).

Foreign buyers and traders were also important sources of technology and market information. Hone (1974) shows that many local firms initially sold their goods to large buying houses from Japan and the US. Some foreign buyers placed orders for 60–100 per cent of the annual capacity of exporters, not only in electronics, but also in clothing and plastic goods. The Japanese buyers (such as Mitsubishi, Mitsui, Marubeui-Ida and Nichimen) purchased huge quantities of low cost goods as wages rose in Japan in the early 1960s, often for sale to the US. Some US retail companies including J.C. Penney, Macy's, Bloomingdales, Marcor, and Sears Roebuck, followed suit.

Wortzel and Wortzel (1981) show how exporters moved from passively selling low cost production capacity to actively promoting their services to new buyers and setting up marketing offices, first at home and then abroad. Foreign buyers supplied latecomers with information on product designs, quality, training and accounting procedures. The largest buyers visited local factories and frequently supervised the start up of new operations. A study by Rhee et al. (1984) indicates that around 50 per cent of firms in Korea (from a sample of 113) benefited directly from buyers through plant visits by foreign engineers. Buyers supplied blueprints, specifications for product designs, information on competitor goods and production processes. In electronics, US retail chains and importers were the most important buyers during the 1970s in Korea. Buyers helped the latecomers to overcome their distance from advanced markets and foreign sources of technology.[16]

OEM, discussed later, evolved out of the joint operations of buyers and latecomers. OEM eventually became the most important channel for export marketing during the 1980s. Under the OEM system, the latecomer produces a good to the exact specification of a foreign buyer or TNC, which then markets the product under its own brand name using its own distribution channels. OEM enabled many latecomers to bypass the need for investing heavily in marketing and distribution, allowing them to concentrate on production. OEM often involved the foreign partner in the selection of capital equipment and the training of managers and engineers, as well as advice on financing and management. Successful OEM arrangements often involved a close long term technological partnership as the TNC assisted the latecomers to improve quality, delivery and price of the final output.

OEM can be contrasted with original design and manufacture (ODM). As the complexity of OEM evolved during the early 1980s, more electronics systems began to be designed and specified (as well as manufactured) by latecomer firms. In 1988–89 this began to be called ODM in Taiwan. The term ODM was first reported by Johnstone (1989: 50–1) who showed that small Taiwanese firms pioneered ODM for clients with no design capability of their own (for example, US chain stores such as Sears). During interviews with SEC and other companies, it became clear that ODM had also evolved in Korea out of OEM arrangements as the *chaebol* acquired capabilities and offered more design services to buyers (Hobday, 1995). This enabled local firms to expand their business opportunities, reduce the risk of relying on low cost labour, and increase value added per unit of sales. Although this was not called ODM in Korea, progress was very similar to that witnessed in Taiwan.

Many informal channels also existed for gaining technology, including the hiring of foreign engineers and the recruiting of locals trained in foreign TNCs. Many engineers went abroad for training in foreign companies, universities, colleges and R&D institutes. The flow of the technically trained back to Taiwan rose from around 250 in 1985, to 750 in 1989 to more than 1000 in 1991 (*Business Week*, 1992: 76). Some firms illegally copied products and reverse engineered designs (Dahlman and Sananikone, 1990). As latecomers grew in size and competence, overseas acquisitions became another means of acquiring technology for firms such as Samsung and Hyundai. Also, strategic partnerships (JVs on a more equal footing) with foreign firms allowed latecomers to enhance their competencies by working on new products and processes jointly with foreign leaders.

In electronics, each of the mechanisms listed in Table 1 was exploited by latecomer firms to overcome technological and market barriers to entry. Some, such as OEM, were dual purpose channels allowing access to both markets and to technologies. The dynamism of the system depended to a large extent on the efforts and abilities of local firms. Some, such as SEC and ACER, led the field, devising new strategies and structures to exploit foreign technology and new market opportunities. By the early 1990s, many latecomers were highly skilled at using foreign market channels as a focusing device for technological learning and innovation.

THE CASE OF SEC OF KOREA

The Chaebol

SEC, widely recognized as the leading electronics company in Korea, is one of three large conglomerates that dominate the electronics industry. The three *chaebol* (SEC, Goldstar Co Ltd. and Daewoo Electronics), which supply around 44 per cent of total electronics production, are fierce competitors spurred on by their mutual rivalry. Goldstar, which in 1958 began producing radios for the domestic market, first exported to a mail order firm in New York in 1962 (Bloom, 1991: 13). By the early 1990s it sold directly to more than 120 countries and boasted nine marketing, and ten manufacturing, subsidiaries, various JVs and five R&D laboratories (Annual Report, 1993). Daewoo Electronics, founded in 1974, began making small cassettes and car radios for export. In 1983 it acquired the

Taehan Electric Wire Company and then diversified into a wide range of electronics products, establishing manufacturing plants in the UK, France, Mexico and China.

In electronics production the *chaebol* are small compared with major Japanese companies such as NEC and Hitachi. SEC's electronics operations are roughly one-quarter of the size of Sony of Japan. However, the sales of the *chaebol* exceed those of most European and US firms (except for IBM and a few others). Also, the *chaebol* are among the fastest growing large electronics companies worldwide. Each has diversified from simple consumer goods to complex industrial electronics and semiconductors. The three firms consistently report operating profits and until the recent crisis appear to have weathered the difficult cyclical downturns which beset other companies. Indeed, during the world economic recession of the early 1990s, the *chaebol* maintained profitability (albeit low) according to official figures, whereas many Japanese, US and European firms sustained heavy losses. The market recession was less severe in Korea's low end areas, while robust local sales helped companies to prosper during the recession.

Other fast growing competitors include Hyundai, Anam and Ssangyong. Hyundai Electronics Industries spun off from the Hyundai Group in 1983. By 1993 it employed around 12,000 and sold more than US$ 1.4 billion in electronics. The Hyundai Group, a massive conglomerate with sales of US$ 54 billion in 1992, built up most of its electronics operations after 1983, partly to imitate the success of SEC. Anam, which began packaging simple chips in 1968, became the world's largest semiconductor assembler with sales of nearly US$ 2 billion in 1993. Ssangyong Computer Systems Corporation began in 1981 as a specialist software developer. In 1988 it began making hardware and by 1993 had introduced its own brand 32 bit microcomputers, page printers and telecommunications systems. With the exception of Anam, each of these firms began as offshoots of existing *chaebol*. Electronics was viewed as an attractive export opportunity both by the family owners of the *chaebol* and by government agencies. Technological advance accompanied growth and diversification and, by the late 1980s, each company operated large R&D facilities. Most had some own brand goods in areas such as CTVs and monitors, camcorders, video cassette recorders (VCRs), microwave ovens, compact disk players, 16 bit and 32 bit microcomputers, telecommunications exchanges, and four, 16 and 64 megabit DRAMs.

SEC's Corporate History

Samsung began in 1938 as a trading company dealing in fruit and dried fish. During the 1950s it diversified into sugar, wool, textiles and other consumer products, responding to the government's import substitution policy. In the mid-1950s the firm began a fire and marine insurance business. Later, in the export promotion period of the 1960s and 1970s, Samsung moved into media (1963), property and retailing (1963), insurance (1963), paper (1965), consumer electronics (1969), construction (1977), aerospace (1977) and semiconductors and telecommunications (1977) (Koh, 1992: 22). During the 1960s SEC was awarded the government's prize of most successful export company in Korea. Since 1977, Group revenues rose from US\$ 1.3 billion to around US\$ 24 billion in 1987, to more than US\$ 50 billion in 1992 (Kraar, 1993: 26). The Samsung Group exported around US\$ 10 billion in 1992, roughly 13 per cent of Korea's total exports. At that time it ranked 18th in the Fortune Global 500 and planned to quadruple sales to US\$ 200 billion by 2002. By 1994, total sales were already in the region of US\$ 64 billion (*Far Eastern Economic Review*, 1996: 88).

Table 2 shows the scope of SEC's activities. In 1992 the Group consisted of 25 companies with assets in the region of Won 18.7 trillion (roughly US\$ 23.5 billion). Although a wide-ranging conglomerate, the Group was a successful international player only in the area of electronics. Other activities, such as chemicals, textiles, heavy industry, aerospace, insurance and trading, were less competitive and confined mainly to domestic markets.

TABLE 2
SAMSUNG GROUP ACTIVITIES (1993)

Activity	%
Electronics	21.7
Financial and information services	58.4
Engineering	9.9
Consumer products	6.4
Social services	2.5
Chemicals	1.1

Source: Samsung, cited by Paisley (1993: 68).

SEC's Performance

SEC began as a JV with Sanyo of Japan in 1969, when it sent 106 employees to Sanyo and NEC for training in the manufacture of radios, TVs and simple components. Under JVs with Sanyo, NEC and Sumitomo of Japan, SEC was able to absorb foreign technology for a variety of consumer goods and components (Koh, 1992: 23). Throughout the 1980s and into the 1990s electronics proved to be the Group's flagship.[17] SEC's sales rose from US\$ 6.6 billion in 1991, to around US\$ 8 billion in 1992, US\$ 10.2 billion in 1993 and roughly US\$ 11.6 billion in 1994, an annual average growth of 25 per cent (Company Reports). Growth occurred at a time when the five largest Japanese electronics firms were averaging growth of zero in 1991, minus five per cent in 1992, and minus three per cent in 1993. In 1995 SEC's sales were expected to be around US\$ 20 billion (just under 50 per cent in chips) with profits of US\$ 3.3 billion (*Far Eastern Economic Review*, 1996: 86).

In 1993 Samsung became the world's largest producer of MOS, selling around US\$2.5 billion worldwide. Largely as a result of SEC's leadership, in 1994 semiconductors became Korea's single largest export, amounting to an estimated US\$8.4 billion (*Business Korea*, 1994: 24). To support its technology development SEC invested massively in R&D. By 1995 R&D spending amounted to around US$ 1.2 billion, roughly six per cent of SEC's turnover (*Far Eastern Economic Review*, 1996: 86).

TABLE 3
SEC's ELECTRONICS PRODUCTION BY SECTOR (%)

	1992	1993	1994
Semiconductors	23	34	36
Information and telecommunications	25	23	24
Consumer electronics	52	43	40

Source: SEC Company Reports.

Table 3 illustrates the growing importance of semiconductors to SEC's sales. By 1994 consumer electronics had fallen to 40 per cent from 52 per cent in 1992, whereas semiconductors had risen to 36 per cent from 23 per cent. It should be noted, however, that within semiconductors the company was heavily dependent on a narrow range of memory products (which accounted for roughly 83 per cent of chip turnover), and DRAMs in particular. During the early 1990s around 70 per cent of total electronics revenues were derived from export sales, mostly due to growth in semiconductors. In 1994 semiconductors accounted for around half of SEC's electronics exports and around ten per cent of total Korean exports of US$ 89.8 billion. However, profitability was low in all but the semiconductor division. Over the three year period 1992–94, consumer electronics and information systems (IS) and telecommunications regularly reported losses (for example, consumer electronics lost US$ 230 million in 1993, but recovered to US$ 39 million profit in 1994; IS and telecommunications recorded losses of US$ 32 million in 1992 and US$ 96 million in 1993 but recovered to US$ 40 million profit in 1994). These losses were more than balanced out by the large semiconductor profits of US$ 960 million in 1993 and US$ 855 million in 1994 (Company Reports).

Innovation Leadership in Semiconductors

Although SEC provides an example of innovation leadership in semiconductors, it also exhibits several remaining latecomer disadvantages in telecommunications and consumer electronics, where it depends heavily on overseas firms for technology and market channels. It is interesting, therefore, to compare SEC's achievements across these three core sectors. Each case proceeded with trial and error exploitation of foreign linkages. New strategies were devised to allow SEC to overcome barriers to entry and to build channels into overseas markets.

As noted above, SEC began assembling simple transistor radios and black and white TVs under a JV with Sanyo Electric in 1969. By the early 1990s it had advanced to technology leadership in chips. In 1992 it became the first company in the world to produce working samples of the latest 64 megabit memory. In 1993 it invested US$ 1 billion in semiconductors, bringing total SEC investments in chips to around US$ 3 billion (Kraar, 1993: 28). In 1992 SEC joined with Toshiba (the world's leading DRAM maker) in an eight year strategic alliance to develop so-called flash memories, a new advanced technology. In 1994 SEC formed a partnership with NEC to swap research data on the 256 megabit DRAM, the next generation semiconductor memory (*Business Week,* 1994: 34). In DRAMs, SEC had become a world leader, overtaking most European and US companies, as well as several Japanese competitors.

SEC's history in semiconductors is one of long term vision, bold decisions, extreme risk-taking, speed, tenacity and trial and error learning. Technology was acquired through SEC's strategy of systematically exploiting foreign channels, often with willing suppliers. Semiconductor development can be divided into three main stages: entry, catch-up and leadership.

Stage 1: Initial Entry

Stage 1 lasted from around 1975 to 1983. It began with initial entry and a fairly long period of learning the basics of assembly. In 1975 SEC acquired the only locally owned chip company in Korea (Korea Semiconductor) which manufactured complementary MOS (CMOS) chips for watches. Although production was expanded, overall the venture recorded losses (Archambault, 1991: 55). In 1980, unsatisfied with SEC's image as a low end consumer goods producer, the then Chairman (Lee), father of the current Chairman, decided to launch the company into the international chip business. He devised a conscious strategy to use semiconductors to upgrade and expand SEC's overall electronics operations. Acknowledging the riskiness of the decision, Lee decided to follow the Japanese example of mass producing DRAMs. Lee visited Japan and the US and set up a team to assess the most effective means of market entry. To acquire DRAM technology, SEC formed a JV with Micron Technology of the US. Micron, which had developed a 64 kilobit DRAM, suitable for low end PCs and volume consumer goods, licensed its technology to SEC and, in return, SEC invested around US$ 5 million in Micron. There were very few trained chip engineers in Korea at that time. SEC, therefore, began transferring young engineers from other parts of its electronics business to learn about the technology from the US firm. Although some senior engineers were recruited from the US, most were hired in from Korean universities. Some of Micron's engineers were despatched to Korea to train SEC's staff under the licensing deal.

SEC also learned DRAM technology by forming a company in Silicon Valley (Tristar Semiconductor) in 1983. This involved an initial investment of US$ 10 million, followed by a further US$ 60 million in 1984. Again, this strategy mirrored the Japanese pattern of investing in Silicon Valley to acquire US high technology firms (for example, Fujitsu's investment in the

Amdahl Corporation). Initially, most of Tristar's engineers were American. However, Korean managers complained of their 'lack of dedication' (*International Management*, 1984: 78). SEC's solution was to hire more US-trained Asian engineers, mostly Korean and ethnic Chinese, who succeeded in producing the 64 kilobit chip and, later, the 256 kilobit DRAM, in-house. In 1984, SEC began production of 64 kilobit DRAMs as well as related products such as the 16 kilobit EEPROM (also licensed from Micron) and the 16 kilobit SRAM. However, these operations sustained heavy losses, reaching a total of US$ 100 million per annum according to one SEC engineer (SEC interview, 1994).

Stage 2: Process Technology Catch-Up

During Stage 2, SEC assimilated 256 kilobit DRAM technology (between 1984 and 1986) and developed its own one megabit DRAM (*circa* 1987–88). Ironing out many of its process difficulties the firm quickly took control of the design content of mainstream DRAMs. During this period, SEC caught up with the DRAM leaders by heavy investments, trial and error learning and intense foreign collaboration. Between 1984 and 1986, the company planned to market the next generation chip (the 256 kilobit DRAM) through Tristar Semiconductor. Some of Tristar's engineers were recruited from Mostek, a major US DRAM company, then facing difficulties. The engineers succeeded in producing the device in-house with Micron's assistance, and technologically the venture was a success. Initially, the 256 kilobit DRAM failed to generate significant returns because of the 1985 market downturn and the subsequent fall in the price of memory circuits. At the same time, SEC gained design technology for another, specialist type of memory circuit (the EEPROM) from the US firm Excel Microelectronics. Both Excel and Micron were facing financial difficulties and were keen to trade technology for financial support (Archambault, 1991: 59).

Despite the accumulating losses and the uncertainty of the market, SEC continued with its strategy of catching up. In 1987 it joined the international one megabit DRAM competition, then mainly contested by Japanese companies. Previous experience had given the company the confidence to compete in this venture with its own in-house technology. In Silicon Valley, SEC had already built a prototype production line for one megabit DRAMs as early as 1985. Again, the decision was taken by SEC's Chairman, despite the losses already incurred and the considerable investment risk, to mass produce the devices within Korea. Most of the capital equipment was imported from the US. According to executives, this venture was fairly independent, not receiving strategic support from vendors or users, though senior Korean engineers were recruited from IBM and Intel to assist with the development. SEC's engineers managed to design a one megabit DRAM suitable for mass production using CMOS technology (the previous two devices had been based upon NMOS, an earlier generation process). Production began in late 1987 and volume shipments started in 1988. By 1988 SEC had invested a cumulative US$ 800 million in semiconductors with little return (Archambault, 1991: 61). Looking back, this was a remarkable gamble for a latecomer firm.

In 1988 the prices of memory chips rose sharply as a strong market upturn occurred. SEC's main product, the 256 kilobit DRAM, nearly doubled in price compared with one year earlier. According to engineers, previous work on one megabit design and production fed back into the 256 kilobit line. Micron, the original technology provider, attempted to license back SEC's 256 kilobit product (SEC interviews, 1993). The 256 kilobit DRAM, which sold in vast quantities, recouped much of SEC's investments in semiconductors. SEC's total DRAM sales grew from just US$ 12 million in 1984 to US$ 400 million in 1989 and around US$600 million in 1990. Major buyers included US firms such as Tandy, Apple, IBM and other computer makers (*Electronic Business*, 1990: 34). SEC's operating profits on total semiconductor sales of US$ 1.4 billion in 1989 reached around US$ 165 million. Eventually, sales of the one megabit DRAM more than recovered SEC's entire investments in chip technology.

Stage 3: From Catch-Up to Design Leadership

During Stage 3 (1989 onwards), SEC gained design parity or leadership in four, 16 and 64 megabit DRAMs, with leading Japanese and US companies. In four megabit DRAMs, SEC overtook most European and US firms and were only just behind the most advanced Japanese suppliers. As before, the four megabit chip was championed by the company's Chairman. Some senior engineers were hired from the USA to work on specific problems. One, Ilbok Lee, had worked at Intel as an engineer. Lee had a Ph.D. from the University of Minnesota and, in 1989, became president of Samsung Semiconductor. Other engineers were promoted from within the company. Some funding (around ten per cent) was provided by the government's Electronics and Telecommunications Research Institute (ETRI) in a collaborative DRAM venture with other companies, but as in the case of the one megabit DRAM, the core effort and investment was in-house.[18] Almost all of the four megabit design and development work was carried out within SEC. In 1989 SEC began shipping its own four megabit DRAMs, just behind the Japanese leaders. Large users such as IBM, HP, Sun Microsystems and NEC purchased the product in huge volumes, providing feedback on reliability and performance. Intel formed an agreement to resell SEC's DRAMs in the US at this time.

During this phase, evidence of minor product innovations in SEC abounds. The company produced a so-called synchronous DRAM (for use in connection with microprocessors) which it licensed to Oki of Japan. In 1989 and 1990 SEC undertook a patent swap with IBM, an exchange of SRAM technology for NCR's ASIC technology, and a JV with HP and Intergraph Corporation for RISC microprocessor development. In an arrangement with Zilog, SEC acquired a licence to produce microcontrollers for use in consumer electronics such as VCRs. To reduce their dependency on Japanese firms, US companies were keen to cooperate with SEC, not only in DRAMs, but also on other products.

SEC's Silicon Valley operation helped to broaden the company's product range by acquiring new technologies. By 1990 the plant employed around 450, of which around 100 were engineers (mostly American; only 15 were Koreans). As well as marketing and sales, the engineers carried out product development work, technology licensing, and materials and capital equipment purchasing. The operation also tested some advanced new products for SEC (such as programmable logic controllers, ASICs and microprocessors) in the US market.

To compete at the world innovation frontier, SEC forged new, more equal forms of partnership with technology leaders such as Toshiba, NEC, TI, Oki Electronic and Corning. With TI, it began a joint chip manufacturing unit in Portugal. With Corning, it began work on advanced ceramics for ICs. In 1992 SEC joined an eight year agreement with Toshiba (then the world's leading DRAM maker) to develop so-called flash memory chips (by retaining stored information when the power is switched off this technology promised to replace hard disk drives). Although ahead in flash memories, Toshiba (which held the basic patent), needed SEC to help establish the technology as an industry standard. These alliances testified to the new status of SEC as a world leader in semiconductors. According to Kraar (1993: 28), in 1992 SEC became the first company in the world with working samples of the latest 64 megabit DRAM. It was reported that SEC had invested US$ 1 billion in semiconductors in 1993 alone and that, in total, the company had spent US$ 3 billion on chip technology.

Strengths and Weaknesses in Semiconductors

SEC presents an unusual example of a latecomer achieving world leadership in a key technology area. The company orientated its entire chip operation towards the export market and acted boldly to acquire and improve upon foreign technology, taking around 15 years to catch up and overtake most of the international players. By 1992 SEC was no longer a latecomer, or follower, but an innovation leader in DRAMs.

SEC created an important imitation effect in Korea. By 1989, the company accounted for around 70 per cent of Korean IC sales. Others, following SEC's leadership (mostly by licensing foreign technology) included Hyundai (19 per cent of sales) and Goldstar (eight per cent of sales). In the early 1990s each of the companies, though still latecomers, had plans to build their own process and design capabilities following the example of SEC.

Despite the advances there were also disappointments. The Chairman's original strategy for semiconductors had been to upgrade SEC's overall electronics capability by the infusion of advanced technology, an aim still espoused in the early 1990s by Company Chairman Lee Kun Hee, the son of Chairman Lee, who originally devised the chip strategy. However, there was little concrete evidence of synergy between DRAMs and Samsung's in-house systems development. The DRAM strategy was essentially an export led commodity venture and very few devices were used in-house (SEC interviews, 1983, 1984). To a limited extent, there were minor spillovers from DRAMs to other chip areas including SRAMs, logic devices and gate array ASICs. In the ASIC area, SEC ranked 19th in the world in 1993. However, in general the DRAM competence contributed little to SEC's strategic aim to develop the design intensive, customized key components in-house for consumer and computer products. The company remained dependent on Japanese and US firms for many of these. In addition, neither SEC nor other local firms were capable of designing and producing the capital goods required for chip manufacture.

More than any other Korean example, the case of SEC in semiconductors graphically demonstrates the effort, risk and expense faced by latecomers who attempt to become world leaders in electronics. SEC managed this in DRAMs, but at great corporate risk. Few other latecomers could afford the systematic long term investments committed by SEC. The case also testifies to the long term nature of SEC's strategy and the company's ability to learn from failure. SEC not only caught up with the innovation frontier in DRAMs, it joined with other leaders to extend the world technology frontier.

Telecommunications: Learning from the Leaders

During the 1980s, SEC sold large quantities of telecommunications equipment into the domestic market. However, it had little export success and lagged behind European, Japanese and US leaders in complex equipment such as public exchanges. Entry began in 1977 when the Korean government urged SEC to respond to growing domestic demand, especially for public switching gear. Prior to this, SEC had little experience in exchange technology except for a JV in 1974 with GTE for private automatic branch exchanges (PABXs), which had begun production in 1975. In 1977 SEC-GTE was formed, largely for the transfer of PABX technology. SEC then acquired the government owned Korean Telecom Co. (KTC) in 1980 to begin work on switching technology. KTC had already established a wide-ranging technology licensing link with ITT/BTM (Bell Telephone Manufacturing) in Belgium. SEC simultaneously began licensing the Metaconta space division switching system (developed prior to fully digital, time division exchanges) from Alcatel of France to supply the local market. In order to learn how to make public exchanges SEC despatched around 100 engineers to ITT/BTM Belgium for training, while 30 or so Belgian engineers were sent to Korea to help set up the switch manufacturing plant at Gumi. Manufacture began in 1980, and by 1993 around four to five million lines had been installed locally. In 1982 SEC renegotiated with ITT/BTM for the transfer of the fully digital (TDS) System 12. The Korea Telecom Authority (KTA) also pushed SEC to secure further technology transfer from ITT/BTM.

In parallel with these efforts, in 1980 ETRI[19] promoted a JV for an indigenous Korean switching system (the TDX) and in 1982 some 25 engineers were sent to Belgium for training in the manufacture of time division mutliplexing exchanges. Goldstar, another collaborator with ETRI, sent engineers to AT&T for training in the US. Both SEC and Goldstar used their longstanding relationships with foreign partners to acquire telecommunications technology and to feed this into the domestic TDX system. The main technology supplier for the TDX system under ETRI was Ericsson of Sweden. Production of the Ericsson AXE digital exchange had began under licence in 1983. Later, Ericsson was involved in the JV called OPC (Oriental Precision Company) with a number of Korean firms. Ericsson helped develop and produce the localized TDX-1 public exchange (10–20,000 line capacity) and transferred know-how for the more advanced TDX-10 (100,000 line) exchange. In the early stages it was difficult, but not impossible, for SEC to hire production engineers. When SEC began it had no specialist engineers in-house. Indeed, prior to 1977, very few Korean engineers had any experience in telecommunications switching. In 1978 young electronics engineers were recruited from SEC and other parts of the Group to begin learning the technology. SEC also poached some engineers from Goldstar, which had a JV with Siemens for the mechanical Strowger systems, and from OPC. Formal in-house technology training began in 1978, but the core learning took place in Belgium with SEC's team of mostly young engineers.

Although several studies stress the importance of government/ETRI intervention in Korean telecommunications, the chief source of technology was foreign firms. SEC and the other latecomers bargained with foreign companies for training and technical assistance inside and outside Korea. As the instrument of the government, ETRI oversaw some of the software development and organized field trials.

Studies of Korean technological progress, especially in telecommunications, often overlook the strategies and skills of local firms in setting up and exploiting foreign channels of technology to their advantage.[20] By viewing company behaviour as merely a 'response' to government policy, such studies can underestimate the capabilities and tenacity needed for latecomer firms to succeed, as well as the strategic differences between companies.

In contrast to semiconductors, SEC is still heavily dependent on overseas firms for core telecommunications technologies such as software and microprocessors and maintains alliances to keep up with technological advances. The company's main export strengths still lie in low end, consumer type equipment such as fax and answerphone machines. In public switching systems, key components (such as microprocessor chips) are imported from ITT, AT&T and other leaders.

Consumer Electronics: Remaining Latecomer Disadvantages

SEC's performance in consumer goods, though very impressive, also lags behind semiconductors in both technology acquisition and brand name recognition. In the early 1990s the company still relied significantly on

OEM channels for distribution and competitors for key components and new product designs. As noted above, SEC's consumer electronics business began in 1969 with a JV with Sanyo Electric following consultation with several Japanese firms (including the Chairman of Sanyo Electric). To acquire manufacturing know-how, the company sent 106 employees to Sanyo and NEC for training in assembly methods for radios, TVs and a range of components (Koh, 1992: 23). SEC learned production techniques under both OEM and licensing deals. In 1981 Toshiba licensed microwave oven technology to SEC. In 1982 Philips supplied CTV technology. VCR technology was licensed from JVC and Sony in 1983. By the late 1980s, SEC had acquired sufficient capabilities to begin joint developments in VCRs with Tenking of Japan (1989), in camcorders with TRD of Japan (1990) and in CTVs with a German company (1990) (Koh, 1992: 22). In 1992 SEC's main exports were VCRs and microwave ovens (treated as an electronics product by SEC). One in five microwave ovens sold in the US were made by SEC in 1992, mostly under OEM deals with GTE.

During the 1980s and 1990s, the company continued to depend on OEM, a reflection of continuing latecomer orientation in this product sector, though own brand sales increased markedly. Own brand sales (excluding semiconductors) in 1989 were around 35 per cent of total exports, while OEM and related sales amounted to around 65 per cent of exports. Thereafter, own brand sales increased to 55 per cent in 1992, to 56 per cent in 1993 and 57 per cent in 1994. OEM and other non-brand sales therefore still represented a major percentage of SEC's exports as recently as 1994 (roughly 43 per cent) (Company Reports). Other large Korean firms depend far more on OEM for their consumer goods sales. In 1990, OEM accounted for around 70–80 per cent of Korean electronics exports (excluding semiconductors), and even more in the latest technology goods (*Electronic Business*, 1991: 59). Earlier, Jun and Kim (1990: 22) showed that OEM constituted about 50–60 per cent of exports of Korean CTVs and VCRs in 1988.

From a technological perspective, much of the design content of SEC's consumer goods is carried out within the company (Interviews with production engineers, 1993). This corresponds to ODM rather than basic OEM (see later points). This shift to ODM occurred in the latter half of the 1980s, signifying that important design capabilities had been acquired by the company. In mainstream goods, most of the detailed design specifications, design–process interfacing and production tooling had been mastered by SEC. However, in more advanced consumer goods SEC could boast few, if any, major innovations. The company had made large efforts to reach the product innovation frontier, but had no in-house innovation equivalent to, say, a camcorder, a Walkman or a colour printer.

For a long time, the company's strategy has been to close the innovation gap through R&D expenditures and deeper foreign technology transfers. For example, it hired 12 Russian scientists to help develop the new digital videodisk recorder (D-VDR). This project used Russian green laser expertise to compress digital data onto a disk space in order to show a feature length film on a 5.25 inch disk. Some 60 researchers worked full-time on the project, which cost an estimated US$ 60 million over three years. Another product developed in 1992 was a low cost (around US$ 600 per unit) colour video printer capable of printing images from a TV faster than Japanese models. This was developed jointly with Kodak. Another element of SEC's consumer goods strategy was to harness the company's semiconductor skills to develop customized chips for systems. However, as shown above, this policy failed to deliver significant results, with most of the chip effort being directed to the commodity DRAM export market.

In consumer goods, SEC lagged behind the Japanese and European leaders in the 1990s and was still dependent on competitors for core components and lacked major, internationally successful product innovations. Japanese firms supplied most of the gas plasma displays (used in advanced TVs), liquid crystal displays (used in laptops and other PCs), charge-coupled devices (CCDs, used in camcorders) and other customized chips. Despite considerable advances, SEC remained a latecomer in consumer goods, relying on OEM/ODM and licensing. In mature products the company had achieved parity, introducing its own incremental product innovations, but it had yet to close the technology gap with the leaders in new product areas. Needless to say, other Korean latecomers lagged behind SEC in this field.

Comparing SEC's Technological Learning Paths

The semiconductor, consumer and telecommunications cases testify to SEC's strategies, strengths and weaknesses in electronics. They show how SEC progressed from simple OEM through to licensing, ODM and joint developments of technology with market leaders. SEC's in-house engineering and R&D efforts helped it acquire, adapt and improve upon foreign technology. Learning gradually from competitors, SEC took a long term strategic approach to technological acquisition, often taking considerable risks.

With the exception of semiconductors, the company remains a latecomer in some important respects, dependent on foreign suppliers for complex software, key components and, frequently, export market channels. In telecommunications the firm relies on outside suppliers for core software skills and for customized chips, though the gap with the market leaders has narrowed through time. In consumer goods too, the company is beholden to its natural competitors on the world stage.

THE CASE OF ACER OF TAIWAN

Taiwan's Unknown Latecomers

In some respects, Taiwan's electronics industry provides a stark comparison with Korea. In Taiwan, electronics relied for its early development on a multitude of small and medium-sized enterprises (SMEs). However, there are also similarities with Korea. The Taiwanese electronics industry benefited considerably from TNC investments, JVs and foreign buyers. TNCs helped to foster the electronics industry, as large numbers of local firms rushed in to supply them with goods and services, leading to a thriving subcontracting and OEM system. In contrast with Korea, in Taiwan FDI continued to play a central part in the electronics sector through the 1980s and into the 1990s.

By the late 1980s the term ODM had begun to be used widely in Taiwan. ODM provided an alternative to original brand manufacture (OBM) for SMEs. Most importantly, ODM signified a new stage in latecomer product innovation, going beyond the processes learned under OEM and subcontracting.

In contrast with the *chaebol*, most of Taiwan's latecomers are unknown in the West, though today they supply a significant proportion of the world's electronics output. In 1994 Taiwan's share of worldwide PC production was around 28 per cent and was expected to reach 35 per cent in 1995 (*Electronic Business Asia*, 1995: 44). Taiwanese firms supply huge quantities of colour monitors, keyboards, mice, image scanners and motherboards (the main circuit board used in PCs). In 1994, computer hardware production grew by around 14 per cent to roughly US$ 10 billion, plus software services of some US$ 1.4 billion.

In all, Taiwan boasts around 700 electronics hardware manufacturers (mostly SMEs) and about 300 software and service companies (O'Connor and Wang, 1992: 53–4). Hundreds of flexible, fast moving SMEs regularly enter and exit the industry. By the early 1990s, the industry had earned itself the reputation of the 'international arms dealer' of the computer trade (*Business Week*, 1993: 36). Firms such as Tatung, ACER and Mitac lead the industry and now enjoy substantial own brand sales. Most others (such as Inventec, Quanta, Elite and Twinhead), mostly unheard of in Europe, rely mainly on OEM/ODM for sales.

Table 4 shows the major US, European and Japanese brand name buyers, the Taiwanese suppliers and computer product lines for 1995. As the case of ACER shows, the progress of Taiwanese firms has been a long difficult struggle, and not without significant setbacks.

ACER's Performance

Each of the firms in Table 4 has its own distinctive history. In computers the best known firm is ACER, established under the name Multitech International Corporation in 1976 with 11 engineers. The firm was founded by industry leader Stan Shih who, as a boy, delivered eggs to earn money. ACER's sales rose from US$ 331 million in 1987 to US$ 600 million in 1988 and then to roughly US$ 3.2 billion in 1994 (*Time*, 1995: 69). In 1988 the firm produced around 400,000 PCs (six per cent of the world market) and employed roughly 4,000, of which 500 or so worked in R&D. This increased to around 800 in 1992. In 1995 ACER was rated by International

TABLE 4
TAIWANESE OEM/ODM PARTNERSHIPS AND MAJOR COMPUTER PRODUCT LINES

OEM Buyer	Product	Taiwan producer
Apple	Monitor	Tatung
	Notebook	ACER
Compaq	Monitor	ADI, Teco
	Notebook	Inventec
	PC	Mitac
Dell	Monitor	Lite-on, Royal
	Notebook	Quanta
	Motherboard	GVC, Lun Hwa, FIC
IBM	Monitor	Sampo
	Motherboard	GVC, Elite, Lung Hwa
	Notebook	ASE
Packard Bell	PC	Tatung
	Motherboard	Tatung, GVC
AST	Notebook	Quanta, Compal
DEC	Alpha PC	Elite
Gateway 2000	Monitor	Mag
	Notebook	ASE
Sharp	Notebook	Twinhead
NEC	Monitor	Tatung
	Motherboard	Elite
Hitachi	Monitor	ACER
	Notebook	Twinhead
Epson	PC	Unitron
	Notebook	ASE, Compal, Twinhead
Philips	Notebook	Kapok
Siemens Nixdorf	Monitor	Kapok
	Notebook	Quanta
Vobis	Notebook	Clevo
	Monitor	Royal

Sources: Electronic Business Asia (1995).

Data Corporation to be the tenth most popular brand in the US market and the seventh worldwide. By 1995 sales had risen to an estimated US$ 5.7 billion, a 78 per cent increase on the previous year (*Far Eastern Economic Review*, 1996: 90).

ACER's technological performance has consistently been impressive. It developed the first Chinese operating system and contributed its own four, eight, 16 and 32 bit PCs. It came second in the world with the 32 bit PC, ahead of IBM and just behind Compaq, and was the first company worldwide to develop a user-upgradable PC, allowing the customer to upgrade the computer by plugging in new microprocessor units. In 1991 it diversified into semiconductors by forming a JV with TI (partly funded by the Taiwanese government) to produce DRAMs within Taiwan. ACER's initial contribution was around US$ 70 million to the US$ 400 million facility.[21]

During the late 1980s, ACER was among the world's largest producers of PCs, colour monitors, keyboards, fax machines and printers. It developed its own brand workstations, operating systems and new chip designs. As a major OEM supplier to Apple, Hitachi, Canon, ITT, AT&T and other market leaders, ACER consistently showed original innovative capabilities. As noted, it designed the first Chinese operating system (called Dragon), which later became a standard in Asia. With IBM, Apple and several Japanese companies, it helped define Asian computer standards.

TABLE 5

ACER: BEHIND THE FRONTIER INNOVATIONS – A SELECTION

1984 – Developed own version of 4 bit microcomputer (later followed by 8, 16 and 32 bit PCs)
1986 – Launched world's second 32 bit PC, after Compaq but ahead of IBM
1988 – Began developing supercomputer technology using Unix operating system
1989 – Produced own semiconductor ASIC to compete with IBM's PS/2 technology
1991 – Formed joint company with TI (and Taiwanese government) to make memory chips (DRAMs) in Taiwan
1992 – formed alliances with Daimler Benz and Smith Corona to develop specialist microelectronics technology
1993 – produced novel PC using reduced instruction set (RISC) chip running Microsoft's Windows NT operating system
1993 – licensed own US patented ChipUp* technology to Intel (in return for royalties)
1993 – received royalties from National Semiconductor, TI, Unisys, NEC and others for licensing out its PC chipset designs.

* allows a single-chip upgrade to a dual-Pentium microprocessing system.

Source: see note 21.

Table 5 presents a small number of ACER's achievements. The firm developed systems and software innovations upon a solid foundation of process technology. Many of the new software capabilities were developed from behind the R&D frontier set by Intel, IBM, AT&T and others. Often, these efforts were funded by revenues gained from low cost manufactured goods sold under OEM. In 1993, up to 40 per cent of ACER's output was sold under OEM/ODM. Many of ACER's original brand goods were intelligently modified and improved PC designs. As Table 5 shows, ACER produced significant innovations, many of which were highly valued by users. Ultimately the company began licensing back technology to leaders such as Intel.

During the 1980s and early 1990s, most of ACER's production was for export, evenly split between the US and Europe. Exports were sold to 70 different countries through a retail network of around 100 distributors. Offshore manufacturing plants were set up in the US, Holland, Malaysia and China. After purchasing Altos in 1980 to distribute computers directly into the US, in 1987 ACER took over Counterpoint, an American supplier of minicomputers. By 1993 its US plant (ACER America) employed around 500 and produced roughly 16,000 PCs a month.

In contrast to early Korean entrants such as SEC, and Taiwanese firms such as Tatung, ACER and other recent entrants benefited from the improving technological infrastructure and the export market channels established during the 1960s and 1970s. ACER was able to enter at a level closer to the technology frontier set by leading TNCs, avoiding the

1960s–70s phase of simple consumer electronics manufacture. ACER quickly began innovating with software, new products and processes for manufacture. Several key engineers and managers benefited from foreign education and from their experience in US corporations. ACER's ability to move from OEM to ODM was also facilitated by its strong in-house R&D effort.

Original Brand Setbacks

In an attempt to challenge brand leaders and move beyond OEM, ACER began to distribute its own brands directly to customers in the US and Europe, while the company's founder and managing director, Stan Shih, began Taiwan's Brand International Promotion Association in an effort to build up Taiwan's quality brand image abroad. However, despite progress in design and branding, ACER still relied on OEM for around 50 per cent of its monitor sales and a significant proportion of its PC sales in 1992.

However, in 1992 the firm scaled down its OBM efforts and retreated to more traditional OEM/ODM after sustaining heavy losses (in the region of US$ 90 million between 1990 and 1993). In 1993 the Group reported a profit of US$ 30 million, partly as a result of the strategy. Refocusing its strategy allowed ACER not only to increase sales and concentrate on production quality, but also to scale back its heavy commitments to own brand advertising, marketing and distribution. Under the new strategy, ACER negotiated one contract worth around US$ 100 million to supply Apple Computer with a popular notebook computer (the PowerBook 145).

Mitac and other rivals of ACER also retreated from own brand sales, focusing instead on OEM and ODM. A chief reason for the general retreat from OBM in Taiwan was the PC price war in 1992, which reduced the price gap between clone and brand name suppliers, leading to large losses across the industry. Mitac, for example, registered a loss of US$ 27.7 million in 1992 (*Electronic Business Asia*, 1995: 44). A second reason was that major US firms, such as HP, began to carefully scrutinize the OBM strategies of their suppliers, preferring to award orders to companies without potential of becoming head on brand competitors.

More recently in Taiwan, the term 'original idea manufacture' (OIM) has come into parlance. Under OIM the product idea is generated by the latecomer, who then designs and manufactures the product, which is then sold under the brand name of Western or Japanese leaders. Companies such as Inventec now use the term 'OIM' to reassure buyers that they have no ambitions of becoming direct, brand name competitors (Inventec, interview, 1994). However, less publicly, many Taiwanese firms believe that unless and until they made a full transition to OBM and in-house technology, they will remain subordinated to the strategies of the international leaders and unable to compete on equal terms.

To sum up, the case of ACER illustrates the vulnerability of East Asia's latecomer firms. Against its desire ACER was forced to retreat from original brand sales after sustaining heavy losses. Early OEM deals allowed

ACER to grow by working as a subcontractor to Intel and others, but this path limited ACER's strategic room for manoeuvre. Under OEM, ACER remained dependent on leaders for core design technologies, market outlets and better known brand names. Its retreat back to OEM/ODM shows the difficulties facing firms wishing to overcome their latecomer disadvantages and compete as leaders.

LATECOMER TECHNOLOGICAL TRANSITION

From OEM to ODM to OBM

In electronics many latecomer companies learned to innovate under the OEM/ODM system. Although each firm has its own particular history, most acquired technology and learned to innovate incrementally, often by imitation. TECO, a major Taiwanese conglomerate, learned under OEM arrangements with IBM and other companies, as did Tatung. TECO advanced from simple consumer goods to computers, colour display terminals, printers, video graphic adapters and TV monitors. By the late 1980s, TECO employed 3,000 in electronics, sales exceeded US$ 300 million and R&D staff numbered in the region of 300.

TABLE 6
TRANSITION OF LATECOMER FIRMS FROM OEM TO ODM AND TO OBM

	Technological transition	Market transition
1960s/70s		
OEM	Learns assembly processes for standard simple goods	Foreign TNC/buyer designs, brandsand distributes
Mid-1980s		
ODM	Local firm designs;* learns product/ process innovation skills	TNC buys, brands and distributes; TNC gains PPVA**
1980s/Mid-90s		
OBM	Local firm designs and conducts R&D for complex products	Local firm organizes distirbution, brand name, and captures PPVA

* Latecomer contributes to the design alone, or in partnership with the foreign company.
** Post-production value added.

Table 6 indicates the progression of latecomers from OEM, to ODM to OBM.[22] Early latecomer entrants began with OEM because they lacked their own marketing capabilities and brand names.[23] By the early 1990s, the *chaebol* and most larger Taiwanese companies had established OBM in at least some areas, though most still depended on OEM/ODM for much of their exports. The linear progression suggested in Table 6 need not occur, nor is there any automatic progress for companies. R&D may begin fairly early on and there may be feedback between early and later stages. Early entrants will tend to begin with simple tasks and develop skills and knowledge in a path-dependent cumulative manner. However, later entrants, such as ACER, may 'jump in' at more advanced levels, missing out the early stages. As the absorptive capacity of the economy increases, new start-ups bypass earlier phases. Spin-offs from older firms and other sectors, as well as new start-ups, constitute the growing industrial base.

Most firms have yet to reach the innovation frontier (defined as the point at which substantial R&D is required to generate new products or processes). This is a moving frontier occupied by world leaders at any given time. However, by the early 1990s, some latecomers reached the frontier in at least some product lines. As in the case of SEC in DRAMs, substantial investments in R&D are then required to compete on the international stage. At the frontier, R&D becomes an early and central part of the innovation process and more traditional leader and follower dynamics begin (Utterback and Abernathy, 1975; Abernathy *et al.*, 1983; Utterback and Suarez, 1993).

The Transition from OEM to ODM

An important transition in Table 6 is from OEM to ODM. Under ODM the latecomer carries out some or all of the product design tasks, often to a general design layout supplied by the foreign buyer. In some cases, the buyer cooperates with the latecomer on the design. In others, the buyer is presented with a range of finished products to choose from, designed by the latecomer firm using its own knowledge of the international market. ODM signifies latecomer internalization of system design skills, complex production technologies and, often, component design abilities.

ODM offers a mechanism for latecomer firms to capture more of the design value added while avoiding the heavy risks and costs of launching own brand products and investing in foreign marketing and distribution channels. Under early forms of OEM, the latecomer would be confined to value added related to assembly services. Under ODM the local company is able to add value in production engineering, design for manufacture and product design. ODM indicates an advanced competence, though it applies mainly to incremental designs, rather than leadership product innovations based on R&D.

Links between Technology and the Market

In Table 6, learning is assumed to occur both at the technological and marketing levels. Firms learn to package, distribute and market their goods (Wortzel and Wortzel, 1981). Some establish marketing departments at home and then in the advanced countries. Marketing know-how enables firms to diversify their customer base and to increase their growth opportunities but, like technology, requires substantial investments in skills and organization. Ultimately, some latecomers establish their own brand names abroad, organize their own distribution and advertise directly to customers.

There may not always be systematic, causal links between the stages of technology and market development. It is possible for a firm to acquire technology but to still remain at the early stages of marketing – or vice versa. However, it is likely that latecomer firms will try and improve both their technology and marketing capabilities simultaneously in order to increase profit and market share. In many cases there are concrete connections and interdependencies between market and technology. Indeed, under OEM/ODM the channels for foreign technological and marketing learning are one and the same. To increase sales to key customers, joint engineering work may be needed, as occurred in SEC and ACER. Later on, to bring new products to the market, firms will probably need to make long term investments in R&D. For successful latecomers, technology and marketing and closely entwined, with market needs acting as a focusing device for learning and innovation.

Advantages and Disadvantages of the OEM/ODM System

Although the OEM/ODM system has allowed latecomers to overcome barriers to entry, the system has several disadvantages. Strategically, the latecomer is often subordinated to the decisions of the foreign buyer and often dependent on a TNC for core designs, key components and market channels. The TNC may impose restrictions on the sales activities of latecomers, while the post-manufacturing valued added may be limited and profits low. Operating under OEM/ODM makes it difficult for latecomers to build up the high quality brand images needed to sell products worldwide.

Despite the problems, it would be wrong to understate the importance of the system in electronics. It facilitated rapid industrial growth in East Asia and permitted the assimilation of technology. More restrictive clauses can be renegotiated, and often are. For example, by setting aside marketing restrictions on more mature products, latecomer firms are often allowed to sell directly into third countries. The system enabled many firms to achieve economies of scale in production, and justified heavy investments in modern automation technology. On their part, foreign market leaders continue to benefit from low cost capacity, enabling rival TNCs to compete with each other. OEM/ODM, therefore, endures as a mutually valued arrangement.

To sum up, within the OEM/ODM system exports pull forward the competencies of latecomer firms, enabling them to overcome the lack of user–producer links enjoyed by leaders and followers. Through OEM/ODM and other channels, export demand acts as a focusing device for learning and forces the pace of innovation. Successful exporters, such as SEC and ACER, are imitated by other latecomers adding to the dynamism of the East Asian electronics industry.

THE THEORETICAL IMPLICATIONS OF LATECOMER INNOVATION

Implications for Modern Resource Based Theories of the Firm

It is not possible from the limited evidence above to generate a general theory of latecomer innovation, nor indeed to know whether a new theory is needed. Such an assessment would require a great deal of evidence from other sectors and other countries and an evaluation of whether existing resource based views of the firm can or cannot deal adequately with latecomer innovation paths and processes. However, it is possible, first, to show how the evidence contrasts with existing mainstream models of innovation and, second, to propose a specific model of latecomer innovation (albeit a simple one), for the case of locally owned East Asian firms in electronics.[24]

The experience of East Asia suggests that it is important that modern resource based theories deal with various categories of firm competing from 'behind' the technology and market frontier. Most modern theories (for example, Teece *et al.*, 1994) and earlier approaches (Penrose, 1959; Ansoff and Stewart, 1967) tend to assume leader or follower status (or potential), both in terms of intra-company resources and the external environment. Such technology resources and complementary assets (Teece, 1986) cannot be taken for granted in developing countries. A latecomer theory should account not only for the disadvantages faced by firms dislocated from advanced markets and technologies, but also their advantages. The latter might include low cost manual, technical and engineering resources. In the case of China, for example, an abundance of cheap technical labour (such as software and mechanical engineers) has enabled many local firms to conduct innovative activities, including the re-engineering and improvement of products and processes, at a fraction of the cost in the developed countries (Hobday, 1995).

At the national level, Gerschenkron (1962) dealt systematically with latecomer advantages and disadvantages but, barring a few exceptions, this has yet to be done at the firm level. A full analysis of latecomer 'positions, paths and processes', to use the terminology of Teece *et al.* (1994), is essential for understanding how and why some developing country firms overcome barriers to entry into advanced markets and why others do not.

Implications for Traditional R&D Innovation Models

Regarding latecomer innovation, the above evidence provides some insights into how East Asian firms overcame barriers to entry in electronics. The strategies and stages witnessed contrast markedly with traditional 'Western' models of innovation, especially those that assume leadership or followership and place R&D, new technology, new product development, corporate visions and market creation at the centre of innovation.[25] In comparison with such models, the path to East Asian competitiveness was catch-up learning and behind the frontier innovation, based on established markets and fairly predictable technological trajectories.

Figure 1 proposes a simple model of the catch up process, the general thrust of which appears to be borne out by the East Asian evidence.[26] In contrast with Western models, the NIEs began with mature, standardized manufacturing processes and gradually moved on to more advanced stages of process engineering, product–process interfacing and product design.

FIGURE 1: LATECOMER FIRMS – EXPORT-LED LEARNING FROM BEHIND THE TECHNOLOGY FRONTIER

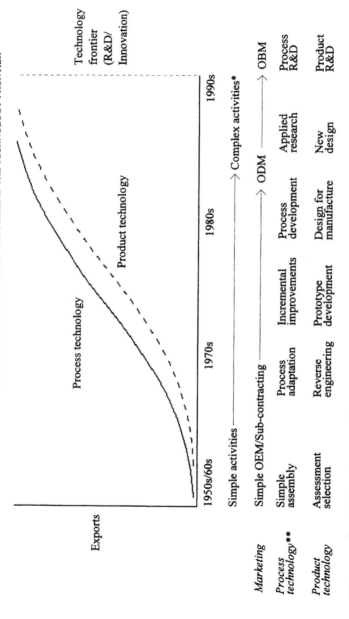

* No stages or linearity implied, but a general tendency to catch up cumulatively, through time with capabilities building systematically upon each other.
** Although it is useful to distinguish between process and product technology for analytical purposes, in practice the two are often inextricably entwined.

Only recently, and only very selectively, have OEM suppliers exploited R&D for new product development. Typically, firms graduated from mature to early stages of the product life cycle, from standard to experimental manufacturing processes, and from incremental production changes to R&D. In this sense NIE firms moved 'backwards' along the 'normal' stages of the product life cycle.

In line with Figure 1, East Asian firms developed competitive strategies in order to compete from a technologically weak position and to catch up. Manufacturing for established export markets under OEM enabled firms to engage in catch-up learning, imitation and innovation, allowing companies to expand exports, to improve their production capabilities and, in some cases, to begin new product innovation, as occurred previously in Japan.[27] This catch-up process appears to be a natural sequence among many successful OEM suppliers in electronics.

Under OEM, latecomer firms engaged in a cumulative incremental process of technological learning, beginning mostly in activities that could be described as 'pre-electronic' in character (such as mechanical, electromechanical and precision engineering). In contrast, with new product development strategies, firms tended to enter at the mature, well established phase of the product life cycle, rather than at the early stage. The route to more advanced design work and R&D was a long learning process, driven by the demands of manufacturing. Even at today's stage, most East Asian suppliers are weak in new product design and R&D, compared with market leaders in the US and Japan.

Implications for Theories of Location of Production

The East Asian electronics case also has implications for traditional theories of production location and international product life cycles, based on strategies of TNCs (Vernon, 1966; Dunning, 1975). Under OEM, latecomer enterprise actively stimulated the relocation of production and deliberately brought about technology transfer from buyers and machinery suppliers. It is highly doubtful that relocation to Korea and Taiwan would have occurred to the same extent without substantial capability building on the part of local firms. It is also unlikely that production and technology transfer occurred as an automatic consequence of an international product life cycle. On the contrary, local firms generated the skills and competencies to enable foreign technology transfer to occur. Local skills were needed to install production capacity, generate productivity gains and improve production processes. Thus, the East Asian evidence adds a new dimension to classical theories based on the decisions and interests of TNCs firms: the role of domestic enterprise in bringing about the relocation of production.

Technological versus Organizational Innovation

Although we have focused mainly on technology, organizational innovations have also become most notably the OEM/ODM system. By exploiting OEM/ODM, this system enabled many local firms to access foreign export channels, overcome barriers to entry and to learn about new markets and technology. As an institutional mechanism, OEM provided a bridge between advanced users in the West and suppliers in the NIEs, forcing continuous improvements upon competing local suppliers. The OEM/ODM system is new to the marketplace and, therefore, constitutes innovation (albeit organizational innovation) in the strict sense of the term. The regional development that occurred under OEM has no obvious historical counterpart and has already proved to be a large scale feature of economic development in East Asia. With the expansion of OEM into China, Vietnam, the Philippines and other countries, the system is likely to continue to bring about rapid growth in East Asia as a whole.

CONCLUSION: FACING THE INNOVATION FRONTIER

The two case studies, together with other evidence on the origins, innovation paths and strategies of latecomer firms, help to explain the advantages, weaknesses and opportunities facing latecomer firms in non-Japan East Asia. Their strategy for overcoming marketing and technological barriers was to couple technology development with export market needs under the OEM system. Other arrangements, such as licensing, subcontracting, JVs and acquisitions were also important. These institutional mechanisms enabled latecomer firms to learn from foreign buyers and rapidly expand their exports. As they climbed the technological ladder, many companies transferred out their labour intensive activities to Malaysia, Indonesia, Thailand and China, leading to rapid growth of electronics in these countries, the deepening of East Asian economic integration and a burgeoning of intra-regional trade.

The evidence on East Asia's latecomers also pinpoints their continuing weaknesses. Only in a small number of areas have new product designs been generated by local firms. In most fields, companies are still dependent on their natural competitors for core designs, key components, capital goods and overseas distribution channels. Despite the advances of companies such as SEC and ACER, most latecomer firms still suffer from weaknesses in R&D and poor brand images abroad. Without stronger product innovation capabilities they will continue to rely on a mixture of catch-up, imitation based growth and incremental innovation.

The majority of latecomers are still distinct from followers and leaders. Although some have made the transition in some areas, most are highly dependent on OEM/ODM for access to markets and technology. As more latecomers approach the innovation frontier, they will require new strategies to gain technology and to overcome other weaknesses. Some may adopt the strategies of leaders by investing heavily in R&D and brand images abroad. Others may attempt to gain advantage by expanding their basic OEM activities into neighbouring low cost areas of East Asia. Already, some companies are pursuing a mixture of both strategies, creating hybrid leader/follower/latecomer corporations, able to combine the benefits of both leaders and latecomers. Such hybrid strategies could prove a powerful competitive formula in the future.

This work has pointed to theoretical implications of latecomer innovation for modern resource based theories of the firm and has tried to show how the evidence contrasted with mainstream models of innovation. It also proposed a simple model of latecomer innovation for the case of locally owned East Asian firms in electronics. There is a need for resource based views to account for the many categories of firms which compete, not as leaders or followers, but as latecomer firms based in developing countries and dislocated from advanced markets and technologies. We also touched on the implications for classical theories of production location and international product life cycles, showing how local firms in Korea and Taiwan act to bring about technology and production transfer.

To continue their successful growth in the future, more East Asian firms will have to overcome their disadvantages in design, capital goods, R&D and marketing. Although the larger companies are investing heavily in R&D and brand awareness, so far the results have been mixed. Some firms were forced to retreat back into OEM/ODM in the early 1990s after sustaining heavy losses in own brand investments. Others, fearful of the cost and risk of directly challenging US and Japanese leaders, have chosen to rein back their own brand ambitions for the time being.

It would be wrong to overemphasize the technological difficulties facing latecomers as they approach the innovation frontier. Instead in Korea current financial and macroeconomic crisis poses a far greater threat to progress than do technological problems. Historically, latecomer firms have led their economies out of the severe conditions of poverty and backwardness that existed in the 1960s. Today many of these firms are fast growing, highly respected international competitors with impressive technological abilities, finely tuned to the needs of the demanding export markets. Despite the problems, their record so far suggests that further, perhaps unpredictable, competitive advances will be made in the future.

ACKNOWLEDGEMENTS

A version of this contribution is also to appear in a forthcoming book on electronics firms edited by Sir Geoffrey Owen and Professor Martin Fransman. The study is part of the UK Economic and Social Research Council Pacific Asia Research Programme (project reference: L32453023 – Technological Dynamism in Pacific Asia: Implications for Europe). The author would like to thank Martin Bell, Norlela Ariffin and Chris Freeman for helpful comments and advice. The normal disclaimers apply.

NOTES

1. From now on 'Korea' will be used as shorthand for South Korea and Republic of Korea.
2. Jun and Kim (1989) and Bloom (1992) provide overall assessments of the electronics industry in Korea. Ernst and O'Connor (1992) examine the general industrial position of the NIEs in electronics, focusing on problems and barriers to entry. The classic studies on East

Asian technological learning by Dahlman *et al.* (1985), Westphal *et al.* (1985) and Amsden (1989) tend to examine general industrial processes rather than firm-level experiences. They also tend not to look at electronics.

3. Samsung first began making transistor radios in 1961, and SEC was formed from various divisions in 1969. By contrast, ACER was incorporated in 1976 when Taiwan's industrial infrastructure was at a more advanced stage.

4. Dodgson (1991: 23) defines technological learning as: 'the ways firms build and supplement their knowledge bases about technologies, products and processes, and develop and improve the use of the broad skills of their work-forces'. Although learning is difficult to accurately measure or to distinguish from other activities, as Malerba (1992) shows, it is central to incremental technical change, productivity growth and product and process improvements. From a research perspective the case studies rely on interviews with company directors and engineers as well as documented evidence to explore how firms acquired technology, the chief foreign sources, key technological milestones and remaining weaknesses and challenges.

5. OEM occurs when a latecomer firm manufactures a finished good for a foreign buyer (often a large international firm, usually termed the OEM). In Taiwan and Korea OEM accounted for a large proportion of electronics exports during the 1970s–90s. It is very similar to other subcontracting arrangements in sectors such as bicycles and footwear (Egan and Mody, 1992). The term OEM began to be used in the 1950s by computer makers who used East Asian suppliers to produce equipment for them. It was later adopted by US chip companies in the 1960s who used the OEM system to assemble and test semiconductors. Today, the term has acquired a variety of meanings. To avoid confusion, OEM here refers to the subcontracting system in which firms cooperate, rather than the buyer or supplier.

6. See Rush *et al.* (1996) for an examination of the effectiveness of government technology institutions such as the Industrial Technology Research Institute (ITRI) in Taiwan and the Korea Institute for Science and Technology (KIST) in stimulating technological progress.

7. After independence from Japan in 1945, around 74 per cent of Koreans were illiterate. Following the 1945–53 civil war, Korea's per capita income was equivalent to Ghana's and Nigeria's. During the 1950s and 1960s, the industrial base was very small and technologically backward. Even today, both Korea and Taiwan lag well behind the advanced nations according to research and development spend per capita, scientific publications, patenting output, and so on.

8. This draws upon Hobday, 1995, which introduces the idea of the latecomer firm to illustrate the specific conditions facing East Asian firms in electronics.

9. Other problems, concerning finance, marketing skills and managerial competencies, may also face the latecomer enterprise. The latecomer may suffer from a lack of capable, related supplier firms, poor strategic thinking and a lack of information on international technology and market trends.

10. These points were first made by Marshall (1890: Ch. 10) in his work on industrial districts, discussed by Freeman (1990). Other classic studies include Vernon's (1960, especially Ch. 5) study of externalities, Lundvall's (1988) work on user–producer interactions and Porter's (1990) analysis of clusters in the competitive advantage of nations.

11. Note that the notion of innovation (or technology) leader and follower refers to a firm's strategy in a specific product area. A single firm might well be a leader in some product fields and a follower in others. By contrast, latecomers will tend to lag well behind across a broad spectrum of product and process technologies.

12. Follower and leader strategies are analysed by Ansoff and Stewart (1967), Porter (1985: Ch. 5) and Teece (1986). Freeman's (1974: 176) concept of 'offensive' and 'defensive' strategies is broadly equivalent to the 'leadership' and 'followership' strategies of Porter and Teece. Freeman emphasizes that technology strategies relate to specific products, as noted above.

13. Some of the theoretical implications of latecomer paths of innovation are touched upon later.

14. For details see Sakong (1993: 232) for Korea, and O'Connor and Wang (1992: 41) for Taiwan (official figures in current prices). In Korea, electronics accounted for around 28 per cent of total exports in 1991.

15. For further details see Dahlman and Sananikone (1990) and Schive (1990) for Taiwan. Rhee *et al.* (1984) examine the Korean case.

16. A similar story emerges in bicycles. Egan and Mody (1992) and *Forbes* (1992) show how US manufacturers and distributors purchased bicycles in bulk from Taiwan and gradually transferred technology. Eventually the Taiwanese succeeded in displacing most of their former American 'teachers'. Much the same occurred in sewing machines where, as with

bicycles, Taiwan soon became the world's largest producer (Schive, 1990).

17. In 1988 Samsung Semiconductors and Telecommunications Co. was taken over by SEC in order to reinforce potential synergies within electronics.

18. It is not possible here to assess the role of ETRI, which is often cited as being important to the DRAM venture. Suffice to say that during interviews few, if any, of SEC's engineers mentioned ETRI, unless prompted.

19. ETRI actually developed out of another institute in 1982, the Korean Telecommunications Research Institute (KTRI), initially set up as a branch of the KIST.

20. Often this is a matter of emphasis, with authors preferring to focus on the role of government rather than firms (e.g. Amsden 1989; Kim and Dahlman 1992; Lim 1992). In a typical study of telecommunications by Kim *et al.* (1992), very little attention is paid to firms and much is ascribed to government policy. However, without the entrepreneurialism of Korean companies, policies could not be successful.

21. Evidence for this section is from interviews carried out in Taiwan with ACER, Johnstone (1989: 51–2), *Business Week* (1993: 38), the trade press especially *Electronics* (1993: 14), *Computrade International* (1993: 72), Chaponniere and Fouquin (1989: 61) and *Time* (1995: 69).

22. Other supporting evidence for this section is presented in Hobday, 1995.

23. It is important to note that the path taken in Table 6 is not a generalizable model of innovation, but is specific to East Asian electronics firms. The model may well not apply to other types of industry or firms. Where similar features apply (fast export growth, labour cost sensitivity, extensive division of labour across national boundaries) some features of the model may apply, for example, in bicycles, footwear and clothing. However, the relevance to other types of industry (e.g. project based systems industries such as aerospace, intelligent buildings and flight simulators) may be very limited.

24. More evidence is needed from other sectors and other countries (successful and unsuccessful) to generate an empirical base to inform a more general theory.

25. See, for example, Utterback and Abernathy (1975), Abernathy and Clark (1985), Clark and Fujimoto (1991), Swann and Gill (1993), Utterback and Suares (1993), Hamel and Prahalad (1994), Chesbrough and Teece (1996), Tushman and O'Reilly (1997), and in the marketing literature Kotler (1976).

26. See Hobday (1995: especially Ch. 4, pp. 55–56) on Korea.

27. See Abegglen and Stalk (1985) for Japanese corporate innovation patterns.

REFERENCES

Abegglen, J.C. and Stalk, G.S. (1985) *Kaisha, The Japanese Corporation.* New York, NY: Basic Books.

Abernathy, W.J., Clark, K.B. and Kantrow, A.M. (1983) *Industrial Renaissance: Producing a Competitive Future for America.* New York, NY: Basic Books.

Abernathy, W.J. and Clark, K.B. (1985) 'Innovation: Mapping the Winds of Creative Destruction', *Research Policy*, Vol. 14, No. 1, pp. 3–22.

Amsden, A.H. (1989) *Asia's Next Giant: South Korea and Late Industrialisation.* New York, NY: Oxford University Press.

Annual Reports (various).

Ansoff, H.I. and Stewart, J.M. (1967) 'Strategies for a Technology-Based Business', *Harvard Business Review*, Vol. 45, No. 6, pp. 71–83.

Archambault, E.J. (1991) 'Small is Beautiful, Large is Powerful: Manufacturing Semiconductors in South Korea', Unpublished M.Sc. Thesis, SPRU, University of Sussex.

Bloom, M. (1991) 'Globalisation and the Korean Electronics Industry', Paper presented to EASMA conference, INSEAD, Fontainbleu, 17–19 Oct.

Bloom, M. (1992) *Technological Change in the Korean Electronics Industry.* Paris: Development Centre Studies, OECD.

Business Korea (1994) March, p. 24.

Business Week (1992) 30 Nov., p. 76.

Business Week (1993) 8 June, pp. 36–8.

Business Week (1994) 14 March, p. 34.

Chaponniere, J.R. and Fouquin, M. (1989) 'Technological Change and the Electronics Sector – Perspectives and Policy Options for Taiwan', Report Prepared for OECD Development Centre Project, *Technological Change and the Electronics Sector – Perspectives and Policy*

Options for Newly-Industrialising Economies. Paris: OECD.

Chesbrough, H.W. and Teece, D.J. (1996) 'When is Virtual Virtuous?', *Harvard Business Review*, Jan.-Feb. pp. 65–73.

Clark, K.B. and Fujimoto, T. (1991) *Product Development Performance: Strategy, Organization and Management in the World Auto Industry*. Boston, MA: Harvard Business School.

Company Reports (various).

Computrade International (1993) 5 Aug., p. 72.

Dahlman, C.J., Ross-Larson, B. and Westphal, L.E. (1985) *Managing Technological Development: Lessons from the Newly Industrialising Countries*. Washington, DC: The World Bank.

Dahlman, C.J. and Sananikone, O. (1990) *Technology Strategy in the Economy of Taiwan: Exploiting Foreign Linkages and Investing in Local Capability* (Preliminary Draft), Washington, DC: The World Bank.

Dodgson, M. (1991) 'Technological Collaboration and Organisational Learning', DRC Discussion Paper, SPRU, University of Sussex.

Dosi, G. (1988) 'Sources, Procedures, and Microeconomic Effects of Innovation', *Journal of Economic Literature*, Vol. XXVI, pp. 1120–71.

Dunning, J.H. (1975) 'Explaining Changing Patterns of International Production: In Defence of Eclectic Theory', *Oxford Bulletin of Economics and Statistics*, Vol. 41, pp. 269–95

Egan, M.L. and Mody, A. (1992) 'Buyer–Seller Links in Export Development', *World Development*, Vol. 20, No. 3, pp. 321–34.

Electronic Business (1990) 25 June, p. 34.

Electronic Business (1991) 22 April, p. 59.

Electronic Business Asia (1995) Dec., p. 44.

Electronics (1993) 22 Nov., p. 14.

Ernst, D. and O'Connor, D. (1992) *Competing in the Electronics Industry: The Experience of Newly Industrialising Economies*. Paris: Development Centre of the OECD.

Far Eastern Economic Review (1996) 4 Jan., pp. 86–90.

Forbes, (1992) 'Bury thy Teacher', 21 Dec., pp. 90–93.

Freeman, C. (1974) *The Economics of Industrial Innovation*. Middlesex: Penguin.

Freeman, C. (1990) 'Networks of Innovators: A Synthesis of Research Issues', International Workshop on Networks of Innovators, May, Montreal, Canada.

Gerschenkron, A. (1962) *Economic Backwardness in Historical Perspective*. Cambridge, MA: Harvard University Press.

Hamel, G. and Prahalad, C.K. (1994) *Competing for the Future*. Cambridge, MA: Harvard University Press.

Hobday, M.G. (1995) *Innovation in East Asia: The Challenge to Japan*. London: Edward Elgar.

Hone, A. (1974) 'Multinational Corporations and Multinational Buying Groups: Their Impact on the Growth of Asia's Exports of Manufactures – Myths and Realities', *World Development*, Vol. 2, No. 2, pp. 145–9.

International Management (1984) Oct., p. 78.

Johnstone, B. (1989) 'Taiwan Holds Its Lead: Local Makers Move into New Systems', *Far Eastern Economic Review*, 31 Aug., pp. 50–1.

Jun, Y.W. and Kim, S.G. (1990) 'The Korean Electronics Industry: Current Status, Perspectives and Policy Options', Report Prepared for OECD Development Centre Project, *Technological Change and the Electronics Sector – Perspectives and Policy Options for Newly-Industrialising Economies*. Paris: OECD.

Kim, L. and Dahlman, C.J. (1992) 'Technology Policy for Industrialisation: An Integrative Framework and Korea's Experience', *Research Policy*, Vol. 21, pp. 437–52.

Kim, C.O., Kim, Y.K. and Yoon, C.B. (1992) 'Korean Telecommunications Development: Achievements and Cautionary Lessons', *World Development*, Vol. 20, No. 12, pp. 1829–41.

Koh, D.J. (1992) 'Beyond Technological Dependency, towards an Agile Giant: The Strategic Concerns of Samsung Electronics Co. for the 1990s', Unpublished M.Sc. Thesis, SPRU, University of Sussex.

Kotler, P. (1976) *Marketing Management: Analysis, Planning and Control*, 3rd edn. London: Prentice Hall.

Kraar, L. (1993) 'How Samsung Grows So Fast', *Fortune*, 3 May, pp. 26–30.

Langlois, R.N., Pugel, T.A., Hacklisch, C.S, Nelson, R.R. and Egelhoff, W.G. (1988) *Microelectronics: An Industry in Transition*. Boston, MA: Unwin Hyman.

Lim, Y. (1992) 'Export-Led Industrialisation: The Key Policy for Successful Development?, Global Issues and Policy Analysis Branch, UNIDO', Paper prepared for Wilton Park

Conference, 14–18 Dec., London, UK

Lundvall, B. (1988) 'Innovation as an Interactive Process: From User–Producer Interaction to the National System of Innovation', in G. Dosi, C. Freeman, R. Nelson, G. Silverberg and L. Soete (eds), *Technical Change and Economic Theory*. London: Frances Pinter.

Malerba, F. (1992) 'Learning by Firms and Incremental Technical Change', *The Economic Journal*, Vol. 102, pp. 45–59.

Market Intelligence Centre (1995).

Marshall, A. (1890) *Principles of Economics: An Introductory Volume*, 8th edn. London: Macmillan.

Nelson, R.R. and Rosenberg, N. (1993) 'Technical Innovations and National Systems', in R.R. Nelson (ed.), *National Innovation Systems: A Comparative Analysis*. New York, NY: Oxford University Press.

O'Connor, D. and Wang, C. (1992) 'European and Taiwanese Electronics Industries and Cooperation Opportunities', Paper presented at Sino-European Conference on Economic Development, May.

Paisley, E. (1993) 'Innovate, Not Imitate', *Far Eastern Economic Review*, 13 May, pp. 64–70.

Penrose, E.T. (1959) *The Theory of the Growth of the Firm*. Oxford: Blackwell.

Porter M.E. (1985) *Competitive Advantage: Creating and Sustaining Superior Performance*. New York, NY: The Free Press.

Porter M.E. (1990) *The Competitive Advantage of Nations*. London: Macmillan.

Rhee, Y.W., Ross-Larson, B. and Pursell, G. (1984) *Korea's Competitive Edge: Managing the Entry into World Markets*. Baltimore: Johns Hopkins Press.

Rush, H., Hobday, M., Bessant, J., Arnold, E. and Murray, R. (1996) *Technology Institutes: Strategies for Best Practice*. London: Routledge.

Sakong, I. (1993) *Korea in the World Economy*. Washington, DC: Institute for International Economics.

Schive, C. (1990) *The Foreign Factor: the Multinational Corporation's Contribution to the Economic Modernisation of the Republic of China*. Stanford, CA: Hoover Institution Press.

Swann, P. and Gill, J. (1993) *Corporate Vision and Rapid Technological Change*. London: Routledge.

Teece, D. (1986) 'Profiting from Technological Innovation: Implications for Integration, Collaboration, Licensing and Public Policy', *Research Policy*, Vol. 15, pp. 285–305.

Teece, D.J., Pisano, G. and Shuen, A. (1994) 'Dynamic Capabilities and Strategic Management', CCC Working Paper No. 94-9, Centre for Research in Management, University of California at Berkeley.

Time (1995) 25 Sept., p. 69.

Tushman, M.L. and O'Reilly, C.A. (1997) *Winning through Innovation: A Practical Guide to Leading Organizational Change and Renewal*. Cambridge, MA: Harvard Business School.

Utterback, J.M. and Abernathy, W.J. (1975) 'A Dynamic Model of Process and Product Innovation', *OMEGA, The International Journal of Management Science*, Vol. 3, No. 6, pp. 639–56.

Utterback, J.M. and Suarez, F.F. (1993) 'Innovation: Competition, and Industry Structure', *Research Policy*, Vol. 15, pp. 285–305.

Vernon, R. (1960) *Metropolis 1985: An Interpretation of the Findings of the New York Metropolitan Region Study*. Cambridge, MA: Harvard University Press.

Vernon, R. (1966) 'International Investment and International Trade in the Product Life Cycle', *Quarterly Journal of Ecomomics*, Vol. 80, No. 2, pp. 190–207.

Wade, R. (1990) *Governing the Market: Economic Theory and the Role of Government in East Asian Industrialisation*. Princeton, NJ: Princeton University Press.

Westphal, L.E., Kim, L. and Dahlman, C.J. (1985) 'Reflections on the Republic of Korea's Acquisition of Technological Capability', in N. Rosenberg and C. Frischtak (eds), *International Transfer of Technology: Concepts, Measures and Comparisons*. New York, NY: Praeger.

World Bank (1993) *The East Asian Miracle: Economic Growth and Public Policy*. New York, NY: Oxford University Press.

Wortzel, L.H. and Wortzel, H.V. (1981) 'Export Marketing Strategies for NIC and LDC-based Firms', *Columbia Journal of World Business*, Spring.

Global Competition and Latecomer Production Strategies: Samsung of Korea in China

YOUNGSOO KIM

As global competition has accelerated, international production by multinational companies (MNCs) from developed countries (hereafter 'established MNCs') with MNCs from developing countries (hereafter 'latecomer MNCs') has been increasing substantially. The former possess strong capabilities in terms of technology, organization and international management, whereas the latter do not. Established and latecomer MNCs are increasingly in competition in both product manufacturing and market location. Global competition between these players is a new phenomenon.

Latecomer MNCs that have gained an international competitive advantage in the export stage of production in their home country often fail to survive when they go into international production. This is possibly because their foreign operations are challenged by established MNCs. In the early 1990s, South Korea's[1] Samsung and Goldstar, which had been internationally competitive until the late 1980s, closed their colour television (TV) manufacturing plants in the US (Choi and Kenny, 1995). In 1993 Hyundai Motors closed its automobile manufacturing plant in Canada (*Wall Street Journal*, 1994), though the company had achieved international competitiveness during the home based production stage. In 1991 ACER's microcomputer manufacturing in the US experienced heavy losses; so did the state owned Singapore Technology Holdings Corporation, which was making wafers for integrated circuits in the US in 1992 (Hu, 1995: 85).

Cantwell (1991) argues that strong technological capabilities generate a competitive advantage for firms involved in international production. Researchers (Wyatt *et al.*, 1985; Archer, 1986) also suggest that many MNCs still believe that technological superiority is the major means by which they maintain their global competitive advantage. At the same time, others (Bartlett, 1986; Bartlett and Ghoshal, 1988) suggest that the organization of technology has become a generic competitive advantage. Technologically and organizationally weak companies embarking on foreign investment are likely to encounter difficulties in maintaining a sustainable competitive advantage.

A dilemma facing latecomer MNCs is how to compete with established MNCs. Their differential capabilities raise important questions: how can

Youngsoo Kim, Director, Australia–Korea Research Association and Director, SAP Contracting.

latecomer MNCs maintain a competitive advantage when pitted against established MNCs that possess superior capabilities in technology, organization and international management, and what are the relevant innovation strategies that allow their foreign subsidiaries to survive and grow in a rapidly changing global competitive environment? This study deals with the case of Samsung's electronics sector's involvement in international production as an example of a latecomer MNC.

Here the focus is on the case study of Samsung Electronics (SEC) and its affiliated firms such as Samsung Electron Devices (SED), Samsung Electro-Mechanics (SEM) and Samsung Corning (SC). The sources for this study are interviews conducted at Samsung, in Seoul in November 1994 and in the ASEAN region and with managers in China during July and October 1995.[2] We provide an overview of SEC's technological capabilities and overseas expansion before examining two external factors motivating international production in China and a brief introduction to Samsung's international production networks in China. This is followed by a description of its foreign subsidiaries' key value added activities such as production, component sourcing, marketing and design and product development. Next we discuss established MNCs' strategic behaviour in capability transfer and development activities. The final section suggests strategic implications for latecomer MNCs for the achievement of sustainable competitive advantage.

SEC'S TECHNOLOGICAL CAPABILITIES AND OVERSEAS EXPANSION

SEC was established in 1969 and began overseas expansion in 1978, setting up an overseas sales subsidiary to support its export activities. The sales subsidiary acted mainly as a liaison office between the headquarters' export department, and original equipment manufacturer (OEM) buyers during the early stages of overseas expansion. During the 1970s, SEC's technological capabilities were limited to assembling TV sets and producing simple components.

During the 1980s, SEC set up production plants in high labour cost economies in the US and the UK.[3] These operations lacked technological capabilities and were weak in product design and development as well as international management capability. Their strength was production capability in assembling standardized TVs, video cassette recorders (VCRs), microwave ovens, audios, and components (see Table 1). One of the main reasons for investing in the US was to avoid strong trade barriers. From the beginning of the 1980s, colour TV (CTV) imports from Japan, Korea and Taiwan became a controversial trade issue in the US. In response, in 1981, Goldstar – SEC's arch-rival in domestic and US markets – shifted their market strategy from exporting to overseas production with the establishment of a CTV manufacturing subsidiary in the US. Threatened by Goldstar's strategic move, only a few months later Samsung made its first

TABLE 1
TECHNOLOGICAL CAPABILITIES AND OVERSEAS EXPANSION: THE CASE OF SEC

	1970s	1980s	1990s
Key activity	Unrelated diversification	Entry into DRAM	Organizational reform
Main sources of capabilities	JV partners and overseas training	OEM, foreign licensing and training	Acquisitions, joint development, strategic alliances and in-house R&D
Level of technological capabilities	Moderate level of production capability (simple assembly of TVs and standardized components)	Relatively high level of mass production capability (TVs, VCRs, MOs, DRAMs)	Advanced production capability (TVs, VCRs, MOs, DRAMs, components)
		Marginal level of minor product change (negligible in product innovation)	Weak in major change capability (weak in design and development)
		No strategic marketing	Marginal level of strategic marketing
		Very weak in linkage capabilities (de-linkage of functional activities)	Weak in linkage capability (de-linkage of functional activities)
		Weak in international management capability	Improving international management capability
Locations of foreign production	US (sales subsidiary)	US, Portugal, Thailand, UK, Mexico	Indonesia, Malaysia, China, Vietnam, India, Turkey, Hungary, UK Mexico, Portugal, Spain
Product items made by overseas subsidiaries		CTVs, MOs, VCRs, REFs	CTVs, MOs, VCRs, REFs, audios, washing machines, CPTs, CDTs, tuners VCR motors, heads/ drums, DRAMs

Key:
CPT = Colour Picture Tube
CDT = Computer Display Tube
MO = microwave oven
REF = refrigerator

Sources: From Bloom (1992); Ernst (1994); author's research.

foreign direct investment (FDI) in Portugal. Subsequently, in 1984, SEC established a CTV manufacturing plant in the US that performed well for several years, but from 1988 SEC began to close this plant.

In 1988 SEC established a new plant in Mexico and also expanded into South East Asia. At this stage, its competitiveness mainly derived from its production capability, though there was growing concern about the need to upgrade design and development capability. Ernst (1994), Bloom (1992) and Hobday (1995) claim in their studies of the Korean electronics industry that whereas technological capability in product design and development is very weak, production capability is strong. SEC became involved in international production despite these problematic technological capabilities. This is somewhat different from the experience of established MNCs, such as Toshiba, NEC, Matsushita, Sharp, Sanyo, Thomson and Philips.

TABLE 2
PERFORMANCE OF KOREAN ELECTRONICS COMPANIES

		1988	1989	1990	1991	1992	1993
Market	Samsung	39.2	43.0	43.7	46.1	44.9	na
share in	Goldstar	40.8	36.2	40.2	41.7	39.4	na
Korea (%)	Daewoo	20.0	20.1	16.1	11.6	15.7	na
Net profit	Samsung	148.8	233.4	102.8	106.8	94.4	190.8
(US$ m)	Goldstar	26.6	26.5	47.4	25.2	33.4	81.0
	Daewoo	26.0	20.5	18.2	18.5	20.9	47.8
Margin on	Samsung	3.1	4.0	1.6	1.3	1.2	1.9
sales	Goldstar	0.6	0.7	1.1	0.5	0.7	1.3
	Daewoo	1.6	1.2	0.9	0.9	0.9	1.0
Return on	Samsung	6.2	6.5	2.4	1.7	1.8	5.6
investment	Goldstar	1.0	-1.8	2.4	1.2	1.9	3.0
(%)	Daewoo	1.8	1.4	0.9	0.9	0.9	1.4

Source: Company documents cited by Kim and Campbell (1994).

During the 1990s, overseas production rose, with an expansion in the production of technologically more sophisticated products, in addition to standardized consumer products (see Table 1). Yet international expansion by SEC proceeded cautiously. Coincidentally, the profitability of SEC decreased drastically, though sales grew steadily (see Table 2): a situation markedly different from that pertaining until the late 1980s. In his study of Samsung's globalization, Lee (1995) argues that Samsung had first to overcome a variety of obstacles stemming from Korea's own historical and cultural circumstances. In 1993 Chairman Lee Kun-Hee outlined the 'Frankfurt Declaration' in which Samsung's 'New Management' movement was launched through radical organizational reform and cultural transformation. This involved three important strategic priorities: (a) quality-orientated growth, (b) globalization, and (c) multifaceted integration. One of main objectives of New Management was to improve coordination and cooperation between affiliated companies so that they could respond to rapidly changing environments efficiently and effectively. At the same time, Lee believed that in order to maintain a sustainable competitive advantage, Samsung would have to upgrade its technological capability in product innovation and development, a feat that would require long term strategic vision.

Until the early 1990s, expansion through foreign production was neither easy nor smooth. The problems were due in part to a lack of cooperation between group affiliates, mainly caused by organizational inertia. As argued by Choi (1995), Chairman Lee Kun-Hee perceived that the root of the problem was embedded in the organizational culture. Samsung concentrated on addressing organizational inertia, which had grown over the 50 year history of the Group, while accelerating internationalization. The speed of overseas investment has accelerated since 1993, as exemplified by international expansion into China during the New Management movement in Samsung.

MOTIVATIONS FOR INTERNATIONAL PRODUCTION AND INTRODUCTION OF PRODUCTION NETWORKS IN CHINA

Liberalization of the Korean Domestic Market

In 1989 import restrictions on consumer electronics goods were removed and global players continued to enter the Korean domestic market, which had long erected barriers to the import of foreign electronics products. From July 1991, foreign retail distribution outlets were allowed to possess up to ten stores that were less than 1,000 square feet in size (June 1992) – far bigger than the 100–130 square feet that local Korean outlets usually occupied (*SEMM*, April 1991). By 1993 there was a plan to cut the average tariff rate to below ten per cent for all imported electronics goods (Bloom, 1992). Samsung was threatened by the inroads made by global players' attacks. An investigation by Samsung of Taiwan's market liberalization (*SEMM*, April 1991) found that Taiwanese producers had lost huge market shares when faced with competition from Japanese well known brand products. The local market share of Japanese brand products increased dramatically in Taiwan between 1986 and 1990 due to domestic market liberalization (see Table 3).

The Korean electronics market was certainly challenged by the increase in imported products (Bloom, 1992). In 1991 imported electronics goods accounted for five per cent of the local market, but that figure was expected to increase to 15 per cent in 1993 (*SEMM*, April 1991). SEC also estimated that 100,000 imported camcorders were sold in 1990, three times the number sold by Korean producers. This was a real threat to Korean electronics firms, considering that SEC, Goldstar and Daewoo were competing to increase their market share by one or two per cent per year. Moreover, Sharp considered entering the market through existing Korean distribution channels. In July 1993, Sony completed a market survey on entry into the Korean market. It planned to open a sales outlet in 1993 and to expand to 14 outlets by 1994 (*SEMM*, April 1991). Furthermore Japanese and European MNCs continued to enter the Korean domestic market.

TABLE 3
CHANGES OF MARKET SHARE BY PRODUCT IN TAIWAN (%)

Product	Origin of Brand	1986	1990
CTV	Taiwan	81.6	22.3
	Japan	18.5	77.5
VCR	Taiwan	56.7	14.0
	Japan	43.3	86.0
REF	Taiwan	59.9	28.8
	Japan	35.5	62.2
Washing machine	Taiwan	46.5	19.8
	Japan	48.7	72.1

Source: *SMM* (April, 1991).

Growing Demand in the Chinese Market

Due to the rapid growth in personal income and consumption in China, CTV demand in the local market grew rapidly more than the growth of other durable consumer products. According to the World Bank (1990), TV set ownership ratio increased to 13.2 per cent (50 per cent in Beijing) in 1988, from three per cent in 1978. In rural China, only about ten per cent of households had black and white TVs and fewer than four per cent had CTVs. As illustrated by the report, annual TV demand in China has continued to increase: black and white TVs from ten million sets in 1988 to 12 million in 1995; CTVs from 14 million to 20.5 million during the same period. Chinese manufacturers were not able to meet all this local demand. By 1986, some 56 factories supplied about four million CTVs, which accounted for about 55 per cent of local demand; the rest were imported (ibid.). At the same time, almost 45 per cent of CTVs assembled in China were based on imported Semi-Knock-Down (SKD) or Complete-Known-Down (CKD) kits. Moreover, VCR import dependency was much higher than that for CTVs. Of the two million units of local VCR demand in 1993, only ten per cent were supplied by Matsushita's CKD assembly plant in China, and the rest were imported (*Nikkei Top*, 1993a).

There were three problems for local manufacturers: under-utilization of plant capacity, cost inefficiency, and low product quality. As a consequence, key components such as glass bulbs, picture tubes, electronics guns, diode yokes and integrated circuits (ICs) were mostly sourced from overseas. For instance, the Xie Yan TV tube factory produced only 1.1 million units, while international competitors produced 1.5 to 3 million. As a result, the unit cost of a CTV set was 70–80 per cent higher than that achieved by international competitors.

In 1985, according to the World Bank (1990), the component price in China was 120 per cent higher than that for international competitors. China

TABLE 4
GLOBAL MARKET SHARE OF SAMSUNG PRODUCTS (1993)

Product	Total sales (US$ m)	Exports (US$ m)	Global market share (%)	Global rank
SEC	10,145	6,678		
DRAM	3,220	3,056	14	1
CTV	915	637	6	6
VCR	687	553	10	2
MO	346	286	15	2
SED	1,527	1,345		
CRT	1.023	915	13	1
SEM	916	639		
DY	90	84	13	1
FBT	101	91	15	1

Key:
CRT = Cathode Ray Tube
DY = Diode Yoke
FBT = flyback transformers

Sources: Compiled from company data; Jun and Kang (1994).

based firms had to pay about three times the price for flyback transformers produced in China than for internationally produced ones. This meant that Shanghai factories imported 75 per cent of their transformers from Japan. ICs and tuners were also nearly twice the price of the foreign components. The rapidly growing domestic market in China was particularly attractive to potential investors like SEC. Although China had imposed higher tariffs for imports of components, SEC was able to establish a vertically integrated production system, producing both components and end products.

Introduction of SEC's Production Networks in China

Due to the low performance of its foreign subsidiaries' operations in high labour cost economies and its slow process of internationalization in South East Asia, SEC now perceived the importance of strategic planning between its affiliated companies in organizing international production activities. This led to a special effort on the part of top management to carefully plan overseas production activities. SEC's international production in China differed from its South East Asian production: it formed and integrated production networks at greater speed, and this enabled SEC to facilitate the timely transfer of the parent firms' capabilities to the subsidiaries. Cooperative relations between affiliated companies had been improved, driven by the 1993 organizational reform. The quick formation of the China based production networks is largely attributed to top management's strategic commitment and leadership (see Table 5).

TABLE 5
SAMSUNG'S MANUFACTURING SUBSIDIARIES IN CHINA (1995)

Location	Name of foreign affiliates	Year of establishment (and operation)	Samsung's ownership (%)	Product items
Guangdong	Dungguan SEM	1990 (1992)	80	Speakers, audio decks, keyboards, etc
Guangdong	Huizhou Samsung Electronics Co., Ltd (Huizhou SEC)	1992	90 (Nov. 1992)	Audio systems
Tianjin	Tianjin Samsung Corning (Tianjin SC)	April 1992 (Aug. 1992)	100	VCR components (rotary transformers)
Tianjin	Tianjin Samsung Electro-Mechanics-Thailand Co. (Tianjin SEM)	Dec. 1993 (May 1994)	80	FBTs, tuners, VCR drums/heads
Tianjin	Tianjin Samsung Aerospace Industry Co.	1994 (1994)	50	Cameras
Tianjin	Tianjin Tongguang Samsung Electronics Co. (TTSEC)	April 1994 (June 1994)	50	CTVs
Tianjin	Tianjin Samsung Electronics Co. Ltd (TSEC)	Jan. 1993 (Nov. 1993)	50	VCRs, VCR decks
Jinan	Sandong Samsung Telecommunication Co. Ltd (Sandong SEC)	1993 (1994)	46	TDXs
Jiangsu	Samsung Electronics (Suzhou) Semiconductor	1995 (began 1996)	100	Non-memory ICs
Jiangsu	Suzhou SEC Co.	1995 (began 1996)	80	REFs, MOs, washing machines and air conditioners

Key:
TDX = time division exchanges

Sources: Compiled from company data; interviews (Nov. 1995).

From the late 1980s, before diplomatic relations between Korea and China were normalized, SEC started to search for international production opportunities in China. In 1992, SEC and SEM began production of audio products, speakers and audio decks, and computer-related components in Guangdong province. At the same time, SEC participated in one of the government tenders manufacturing VCR deck mechanism units at Dalian, but ultimately lost the tender to Matsushita. Fortunately, the state run electronics manufacturing firm in Tianjin, Tianjin Broadcasting Corporation (TBC), expressed interest in forming a VCR manufacturing joint venture

(JV) with SEC. In April 1993, Tianjin Samsung Electronics Co (TSEC) was approved to begin operations, and in June started production of VCRs in the TBC factory. Subsequently, SEM joined this project, manufacturing core components for VCRs. TBC was also interested in joint production of CTVs with SEC and formed a new JV. SEC also plans to produce microwave ovens, washing machines, refrigerators and non-memory ICs in Suzhou. SEC quickly established an integrated production network in Tianjin for the production of VCRs by TSEC, core components of VCRs by Tianjin SEM, CTVs by Tianjin Tongguang Samsung Electronics Co. (TTSEC) and rotary transformers by Tianjin SC. Tianjin SEM sells TTSEC tuners and TSEC VCR drums, motors and VCR heads. In addition, Tianjin SC supplies Tianjin SEM rotary transformers for the assembly of VCR drums (see Figure 1). SEC has thus established a vertically integrated production system, joining a number of the Group affiliated firms such as SC, SEM, SED and SEC. SEC has also established a JV producing time division exchanges (TDXs) in Shandong.

FIGURE 1
SAMSUNG'S VERTICAL PRODUCTION NETWORK IN TIANJIN, CHINA

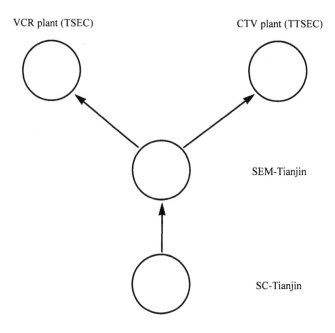

Source: Compiled from company data and interviews (Nov. 1995).

In December 1995, SED decided to produce CRTs for delivery to TTSEC in Tianjin. SC is also planning to build a plant near the subsidiary of SED to produce glass bulbs for use in CRT production. In Suzhou, SEC's semiconductor plant was approved for the production of ICs such as transistors used for consumer electronics products, and these components can also be used by TTSEC, TSEC in Tianjin and Huizhou-SEC in Suzhou. As SEC extended its production networks in China, small and medium-sized Korean components suppliers increased their operation nearby, and they also linked locally with other Korean end product manufacturers, such as Goldstar and Hyundai, operating in China.

FOREIGN SUBSIDIARIES' KEY VALUE ADDED ACTIVITIES

This section overviews foreign subsidiaries' operations related to key value added activities such as production, component sourcing, marketing and design and product development.

Rapidly Growing Production and Adaptation

SEC-run manufacturing subsidiaries in South East Asia found it hard to achieve economies of scale in their early stage of operations. In contrast, the subsidiaries in China were able to maximally utilize the plants from the beginning. In November 1995, TSEC achieved a high plant utilization ratio, over 70 per cent of the existing capacity that was newly built in early 1995, producing 450,000 VCR units. TTSEC grew remarkably in its first years of operation: it increased its production volume from 600,000 sets in 1994, to 800,000 in 1995, and to 1.2 million in 1996.

Most of SEC's subsidiaries were able to utilize local labour, which had accumulated a moderate degree of production capability in the electronics sector over the previous couple of years. TBC, the JV partner of TTSEC and TSEC, had been undertaking production of CTVs for over 30 years before it cooperated with SEC. The JV partners of Tianjin SEM and Tianjin SAI also had broad experience in electronics goods manufacture: the former undertook the production of tuners, and the latter manufactured cameras. This also applies to Shandong-SEC, which is producing TDXs, and to a new CRT manufacturing subsidiary at Shenzhen.

This is in marked contrast to SEC's subsidiaries which were established earlier in the ASEAN region, where most of the JV partners had no experience in manufacturing electronics goods. In addition, most of the subsidiaries were not engaged in greenfield investment, but joint production with Chinese partner companies in which SEC provides up to date equipment, such as chip mounting machines and automatic soldering machines, to the Chinese partners who lack such technological capacity. This means that SEC introduced new technology and the replacement of old machinery and equipment with more advanced ones, guaranteeing improved products as well as higher productivity.

Subsidiaries in China have also been advantaged by utilizing the improved international management capability accumulated through SEC's previous operations. Prior to establishing TTSEC, SEC accumulated international production experience throughout its operations in Portugal, the US, Mexico and Thailand. Similarly, SEC gained knowledge in the international production of VCRs in Spain and Indonesia before the actual production of TSEC began. At the same time, the subsidiaries have easy access to Chinese and Korean speaking ethnic Korean labour. All subsidiaries employ a certain proportion of ethnic Korean personnel to lessen the risk of communication problems.

Continuous Adaptation

All SEC subsidiaries adapt their production system so that they fit into the local socio-economic environment and to ensure the efficient operation of their plants. TSEC installed a flexible production system in which all VCR products are manufactured by the same production line, regardless of whether the products being produced are for export or local distribution. The system is not exactly the same as the one in the headquarters' production plant, but has been modified to fit in with the Chinese local environment. For instance, TSEC's production line has put in more labour than the Korean based VCR plant, not only because of the different levels of automation but also because of the different skills of assembly workers. In addition, the headquarters' process innovation teams visit TSEC and other overseas plants, and make adaptations to the existing production system.

Adaptation also applies to the human resource management (HRM) systems. The employee incentive system brought from the Korean based plant is under substantial modification. One of the Korean managers acknowledges (interview) that:

> We applied the incentive system based on individual worker's performance that had functioned well in Korea to China at the beginning of the operation, but we soon realized that it did not work out properly, and led to increasing complaints amongst a group of workers. In the end, we withdrew it, and the system is under modification in order to fit the local environment in a relevant manner.

Acknowledging socio-economic differences between Korea and China, most subsidiaries also shifted their HRM strategies so that Chinese managers were fully authorized to supervise Chinese workers (for greater details of HRM in the region, see contributors to Rowley, 1998).

Component Sourcing: A Source of SEC's Competitiveness

SEC-run CTV, audio and VCR projects cooperated fairly well with their affiliated component manufacturers. SEC and SEM jointly set out international production strategies so that SEC-run subsidiaries (TSE, TTSEC and Huizhou-SEC) could purchase the components of SEM-run subsidiaries locally (Tianjin SEM and Dongguan SEM) from the beginning of the operation.

The component subsidiaries grew remarkably quickly. Production capacity of five of the seven products made by Tianjin SEM increased from August to December 1995 (see Table 6). Dongguan SEM, which produced audio and computer related components, expanded its production capacity by the establishment of a second plant nearby due to increased market demand. Similarly, Tianjin-SC and Tianjin-SEM grew rapidly, maximally utilizing their plant capacity. Subsequently, VCRs, audios and CTVs made by SEC-run subsidiaries in China became competitive because low cost component sourcing was available in the local market. Suzhou SEC, which will be producing microwave ovens, refrigerators, air conditioners and washing machines, was able to purchase competitive components from Tianjin SEM after it started operations in 1996. When SED's Shenzhen-based subsidiary starts production of CRTs, TTSEC will further reduce its CTV production costs. The component subsidiaries achieved optimal plant utilization despite the fact that the Chinese market was not large enough to consume all of their components. This is because the headquarters played an important role in the coordination of China based manufacturing subsidiaries, plants in Korea and SEC-run foreign subsidiaries (see Figure 2).

TABLE 6
EXPANSION OF PRODUCTION CAPACITY (Tianjin SEM)

Product	Capacity	
	Aug. 1995	Dec. 1995
Drums	200,000	300,000
Heads	600,000	600,000
Tuners	270,000	360,000
FBTs	150,000	150,000
DMT	300,000	500,000
CMT	300,000	500,000
RF MOD	50,000	150,000

Source: interviews (Nov. 1995).

In November 1995, Tianjin SC was assembling rotary transformers and selling 30 per cent of its products locally. The rest was being exported to Korea where the components were being redistributed to SEC's VCR plants in Korea and SEC-run overseas subsidiaries such as SME (Indonesia), TSE (Thailand) and SESA (Spain). Usually, the headquarters' function was to initiate international marketing sales activities on behalf of the manufacturing subsidiaries.

FIGURE 2
SAMSUNG'S INTRA-FIRM COOPERATION IN CHINA AND SOUTH-EAST ASIA:
THE FLOW OF COMPONENTS AND PARTS

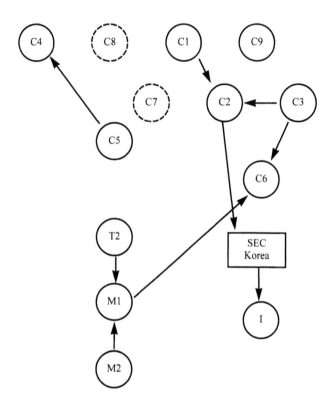

M1:   SED-Malaysia (CPTs, 1991)
M2:   SC-Malaysia (CRT, glass bulbs, 1992)
I: SME (VCRs and audio products, 1991)
T2:   SEM-Thailand (CTV and VCR components, 1990)
C1:   SC-Tianjin (rotary transformers, 1992)
C2:   TSEC (VCRs, VCR decks and VCR drums, 1993)
C3:   SEM-Tianjin (VCR drum motors, tuners, 1993)
C4:   Huizhou SEC (audio products, 1992)
C5:   SEM-Dongguan (speakers, keyboards, etc., 1990)
C6:   TTSEC (CTVs, 1995)
C7:   SSESC (semiconductors, 1995)
C8:   Suzhou SEC (REFs, MOs, washing machines and air conditioners, 1995)
C9:   Samsung Aerospace Industries (cameras, 1994)

Notes: 1. M = Malaysia, T = Thailand, I = Indonesia, C = China
        2. The two FDI projects in Suzhou (C7 + C8) have not been realised, but Samsung
        bought 33 hectares of a Suzhou industrial complex and plans to invest more thanUS$
        500 million for integrated electronics products from components to end-products
        (*Business Times*, 1994)

Sources:SEC (1989, 1995a, 1995b); SED (1990); SC (1994); SMM (Jan. 1988–Dec. 1994);
        SEMM (Jan. 1990–Dec. 1994) and fieldwork undertaken during July and November
        1995.

An average of 70 per cent of the products made by Tianjin SEM was sent to the headquarters in Korea, where some of the products were delivered to SEC-Korea plants manufacturing VCRs and computers and to overseas subsidiaries such as SME in Indonesia. SEM-Dongguan distributes 20 per cent of its components locally, of which a proportion of the audio components were sent to Huizhou-SEC in Guangdong and the majority of audio decks and keyboards for computers were exported to Korea. Tianjin SEM and Tianjin SC distributed about 30 per cent of their total products to the local Chinese market, while the rest (70 per cent) were sent to Korea. The local market expansion is essential to their future growth under SEC's regional strategy for the establishment of component manufacturing subsidiaries in South East Asia, China, North America and Europe.

Marketing: Combination of Local and Global Strategies

VCRs, CTVs and audio systems manufactured by TSEC, TTSEC and Huizhou SEC were distributed to local, regional and global markets in coordination with related global networks. These include the headquarters' marketing function, SEC-owned global sales subsidiaries, OEM buyers, and Chinese local distributors. By November 1995, although the local market share had gradually increased, global and regional market dependency was still high for CTVs and VCRs (40 per cent), audio products (85 per cent), and cameras (90 per cent). However, it is expected that the local market share will increase over time.

Like other subsidiaries in South East Asia, all SEC subsidiaries (except Shandong SEC), did not distribute products to the regional and global markets independently, but relied on headquarters. SEC-Korea's international marketing division is still responsible for the sale of end products and distribution of goods on behalf of foreign subsidiaries.

Centralized Interaction between Headquarters' International Marketing Function and Foreign Subsidiaries

There are two weaknesses in SEC's inter-functional cooperation and interaction. First, most marketing resources and capabilities, as well as the decision making power, have resided, to a large extent, with the headquarters. As a result, interaction between the subsidiaries' marketing function and the overseas distribution channels – either SEC's own marketing subsidiaries or OEM buyers – was rare. This meant that there was little feedback in the form of 'on the spot' information on changing customers' needs relating to the manufacturing and design and development functions of the subsidiaries.

Second, less attention was paid to the expanding Chinese local distribution and service channels than was the case in SEC's Japanese counterparts such as Matsushita. It is important to note that all end product subsidiaries are JVs. Chinese partners are mostly state run companies that lack access to sufficient foreign exchange. Accordingly, they tend to seek short term profits rather than long term growth of subsidiaries. For instance,

TSEC as a newcomer in the VCR market in China obviously needs a huge capital investment in the expansion of distribution, service and advertising. Its long term objective is to become a subsidiary with a production target of 1.4 million VCRs and a local market share up to 20 per cent by the year 2000, up from only four per cent in 1995. TSEC partly depended on headquarters for its advertising expenditure during the early stages of operation. Around 60 per cent of CTV products made by TTSEC were sold through local wholesale distributors under a Beijing brand name, but SEC branded CTVs were planned to be distributed to the local market. This would require additional capital investment for local market development in response to measures taken by established MNCs, which are continuing to expand their local marketing and service channels.

Regional Strategy and Decentralized Interaction

The volume of SEC products exported to America and Europe will not continue to grow as rapidly as recently because SEC's UK and Mexico based regional production networks will soon serve their own regional markets. The Mexico based CTV plant was about to increase its production of CTVs to one million units. Microwave ovens exported to Europe from a Malaysia based manufacturing subsidiary will be gradually replaced by products from the UK based plant, which commenced production in the late 1995.[4] Thus, the local and regional market is of growing importance and this would require strategic marketing. If manufacturers are to meet the local and regional market demand properly, manufacturing, distribution, design and development need to be closely coordinated (see Table 7).

Global market distributors (including both SEC's own sales subsidiaries and OEM buyers) also require multiproduct models with small lot volumes per shipment due to the demands of global distributors' quick delivery systems. This was demonstrated by the difficulties faced by a Malaysia-based SEC microwave oven plant in adapting to changes to GE's distribution and delivery system (interviews, July 1995). Closer cooperation and interaction between overseas manufacturing subsidiaries and global distributors has gradually been increasing and has brought additional pressure with it.

Design and Product Development: Largely Dependent on Headquarters

In contrast to the subsidiaries located in South East Asia, some of the subsidiaries such as TSEC and TTSEC in China possessed their design and development functions within the plants. In fact, TTSEC's design and development function is not SEC's, but the one inherited from the partner company that was recently taken over by TTSEC. With a relatively short history of joint operation, however, it was not possible to conduct independent design and development activities because locally qualified engineers and designers were not available. Despite the existence of a local design function, whenever TTSEC needed new products it had to depend on the headquarters' design and development function.

TABLE 7
REGIONALLY INTEGRATED PRODUCTION NETWORKS (1995)

Region	SEC	SED	SEM	SC
AFTA	Indonesia (CDPs, VCRs REF)	Malaysia (CPTs, CDTs)	Thailand (FBTs, DYs, tuners)	Malaysia (glass bulbs)
	Thailand (CTVs, VCPs, washing machines)			
	Malaysia (MOs)			
CHINA	Tianjin (CVTs, VCRs)		Tianjin (VCR components)	Tianjin (rotary transformers)
	Huizhou (CDPs)			
	Weihai (TDXs)		Guangdong (CCs)	
EUROPE	Hungary (CVTs)	Germany (CPTs)	Portugal (FBTs)	Germany (glass bulbs)
	UK (CTVs)			
	Spain (VCRs)			
	Czech Republic (REFs)			
	Turkey (CTVs)			
	Portugal (DRAMs)			
NAFTA	Mexico (CTVs)		Mexico (CPTs)	Mexico (FBTs, tuners)
	Brazil (CTVs)			

Key:
CPT = Colour Picture Tube
CC = computer components
FBT = Flyback Transformer
VCP = Video Cassette Player

Source: compiled from *Korea Economic Daily* (1995)

Soon after TTSEC joined CTV production with TBC in 1994, several local designers were sent to SEC-Korea to develop a 21 inch CTV for the local Chinese market. The approach taken was to develop the CTV by slightly modifying the previous SEC-Korea model which was exported to the global market for Chinese market conditions. TTSEC's local designers and engineers participated in the project, providing local market information. Even a minor change in product capability was not the function of the subsidiary but of the headquarters, despite the fact that over 100 local designers were working on design and product development. In contrast, TSEC's design and development function, having few local Chinese engineers, placed importance not on product innovation and modification but on increasing local component sourcing. TSEC also sent its local Chinese designers to SEC-Korea for training.

China-based subsidiaries are more advanced in design and development activities than are SEC's subsidiaries in South East Asia. However, centralized design and product development activities are common features in both production networks. This will be an obstacle to product innovation and development capability, which is essential to meet changing local customers' preferences. In a unique departure from this practice, Tianjin Samsung Aerospace Industry was actively involved in camera product development activities in cooperation with local research and development (R&D) laboratories. It contracted with a Tianjin based university R&D laboratory for the development of a low end camera model, at the half the cost of a comparable development in Korea.

As one manager acknowledges, the electronics goods market in China has been shifting rapidly from a sellers' to a buyers' market. It is important to determine the customer's needs and to pass on this information to those responsible for design and development. This enables a firm to shorten product development time and assists with gaining a commercial edge. Recently, SEC introduced a new product, Karaoke TV, to the Chinese market, but sales performance was poor. The new product was originally developed and manufactured by the headquarters in Korea. Although several Korean based designers and engineers visited China for market research and product planning, unit sales were far less (60,000) than forecast (2–300,000). It appears that the product did not really meet local customers' taste. This lesson shows that China-based subsidiaries are under increasing pressure to develop new products near the market place where on the spot information is quickly fed back to production, marketing and design and development functions.

However, it is not always easy for subsidiaries to strengthen their design and development functions. Consensus and understanding are always necessary between both JV partners. There is also a need for additional capital investment, and more Korean designers need to be stationed at the subsidiary, thus increasing the operating costs. From the perspective of financially weak local JV partners, reinforcing design and development functions may not be their major concern and interest. The current discussion on establishing a joint R&D function between TTSEC and TSEC exemplifies this problem.

Decision making undertaken at headquarters has been gradually decentralized to the China-based regional headquarters, in line with the New Management movement. However, most of the design resources and capabilities have remained at the headquarters or overseas design centres outside China and South East Asia (see Table 8). By November 1995, no China-based subsidiaries had established links with the Samsung design Centre in the US, Japan or Germany, nor was there any interaction with foreign firms allied with SEC, or foreign design and development firms acquired by SEC in the early 1990s.

TABLE 8
SEC's OVERSEAS DESIGN CENTRES

Location	Activity	Established
Tokyo	Product design	1987
Osaka	Product design of audio and visual products	1991
Germany	Product design of audio, visual products and home appliances	1992
US	Design of consumer electronics products	1994

Source: SEC, 1995a.

ESTABLISHED MNCS' STRATEGIES

Rapid Transfer of Technological Capabilities

A number of new global players have entered the Chinese market through international production, and existing foreign subsidiaries have continuously expanded their production networks, from end products to manufacturing components and materials. Both SEC subsidiaries currently producing audio and visual products and the ones that are scheduled to manufacture products such as microwave ovens, washing machines and refrigerators from 1996, will face strong competitive pressure from Japanese, American and European MNCs. Japanese MNCs have accelerated the transfer of their technological capability to China, while extending their international production networks in Asia. Recent international production projects undertaken by Matsushita include: washing machines in Zhejiang province (*Nikkei Top*, 1992a); 200,000 CTVs annually in Jinan, Shandong Province from late 1996 (*Nikkei Top*, 1995b); automobile compact disc players aimed at the South East Asian market to be produced in Dalian from October 1995 (*Nikkei Top*, 1995a); and papers in Beijing (*Nikkei Top*, 1992b). The washing machines were in direct competition with those Suzhou SEC was scheduled to produce, while the CTVs will compete with those that TTSEC was already producing.

In addition, the production of microwave ovens and their core component, magnetrons, in Shanghai was scheduled to begin: the former has a capacity of 300,000 ovens, and the latter a capacity of one million magnetrons annually (*Nikkei Top*, 1994a). Matsushita also started production of cellular phones in Beijing, where Motorola held 60 per cent of the Chinese market. Matsushita engaged in international production (*Nikkei Top*, 1993b), while SEC products were made only in the Korean based plant. Beijing Matsuhista Colour CRT Co., incorporated in 1989, began the manufacture of 29 inch CRTs for the local Chinese market with an initial capacity of 350,000 units a year (*Nikkei Industrial News*, 1993a), in addition to the production of 14, 18 and 21 inch CRTs. That amounts to 1.8 million CRTs annually (*Nikkei Industrial News*, 1992).

Pressures to Deepen Production Networks, and towards Decentralized R&D Activities

Since the establishment of VCR deck mechanism production subsidiaries in Dalian, which started operations in 1994, Matsushita has been producing VCRs heads, cylinders and other core components equivalent to 1.5 million VCRs in China (*Nikkei Industrial News*, 1993b). All nine local Chinese VCR makers have purchased VCR key components almost exclusively from Matsushita, a VCR industry leader in China (ibid.). Furthermore, a new JV started operations in October 1995 producing ICs for domestic VCRs (*Nikkei Top*, 1994c). Apart from deepening its vertical production networks, Matsushita has strong bargaining power in China for the further expansion of production networks, as a result of its alliance with the Chinese Ministry of Radio, Film and Television (*Nikkei Top*, 1992c). In order to support its 16 manufacturing subsidiaries and one sale subsidiary located in China, Matsushita established a direct management service network in China and opened an office in 12 provinces, as well as establishing a training centre for service engineers in Beijing (*Nikkei Top*, 1991a). It will also set up a production support system to provide staff training, business consulting, sales and services, market surveys and advertising services (*Nikkei Top*, 1994b).

SEC's competitive position in China has been strongly challenged by established MNCs. While SEC produces magnetrons in Korea only, Matsushita manufactures them locally. Suzhou-SEC only started production of air conditioners in 1996, while Matsushita commenced production of 300,000 rotary compressors (the core component of air conditioners) in January 1995. Mitsubishi will be producing air conditioners from January 1998 and Hitachi will increase their production volume from, 400,000 to 1.4 million by 1998 (*Nikkei Industrial News*, 1995). SEC has been continuously under pressure to transfer the technological capability of the more sophisticated components and materials quickly in response to strategic moves by established MNCs that have not only maintained a vertical production network but also introduced prestigious brand names into the local Chinese market.

In addition to design and development laboratories created by established MNCs in South East Asia, R&D laboratories have also been closely coordinated with China-based subsidiaries (see Table 9). Japanese MNCs have continued to upgrade their product change capability through cross functional cooperation and interactions between manufacturing, marketing and service, and design and development in China.

TABLE 9
JAPANESE ELECTRONICS MNC'S DESIGN AND PRODUCT DEVELOPMENT ACTIVITIES IN
SOUTH EAST ASIA

	Singapore	Malaysia	Thailand
Comprehensive	Toshiba, Hitachi, Mitsubishi Electric, NEC		
Consumer	JVC, Sony, Matsushita	Matsushita Electric, JVC, Sony, Sharp	Sanyo
Audiovisual	Aiwa		Sanyo
Components	Nemic-Lambda, Matsushita Denshi, Kami Electrics Industry, Taiyo Yuden	Nemic-Lambda, TDK, Omron	Matsushita Denshi

Sources: Compiled from data in *Jukagukogyo Tsashinsha* (1992); *Asia no denshi kogyo* (1993 edn), cited by Baba and Hatashima (1995).

In addition, Toshiba and Matsushita have started to strengthen customer service for home appliances in China. Moreover, inter-government coordination between China and Japan has also increased, with the establishment of a R&D support system in China: the Chinese Academy of Sciences and Japan's MITI (Ministry of International Trade and Industry) planned to open a China based advanced R&D centre, which will be engaged in developing and manufacturing computer software in Zhuhai, Guangdong province. This facility will involve major financial investment and the recruitment of 2–3,000 engineers (*Nikkei Top*, 1991b).

TABLE 10
OVERSEAS PRODUCTION RATIO (UNIT QUANTITY PRODUCED OVERSEAS DIVIDED
BY TOTAL PRODUCED)

		1992	1993	1994	1995
CTV	Samsung	27	33	36	41a
	Japanese electronics firms	67	72	86b	na
VCR	Samsung	16	18	20	27a
	Japanese electronics firms	36	48	71c	83c

Key:
a = forecast.
b = Sharp's overseas production ratio.
c = actual overseas production ratio in 1994 Sanyo's 1995 forecast.

Sources: Electronics Industry Association of Japan (EIAJ); Tsuda and Shinada (1995); *Junja-Shinmun* (1993); *Hankuk-Ilbo* (1995), *Chosun-Ilbo* (1995).

As noted earlier, SEC's product innovation and development is not as strong as that of its Japanese counterparts. This is due to weakness in design capability (see Figure 3). Besides, the overseas production ratio is much lower than that of Japanese counterparts (see Table 10). This means that more products are dependent on Korean-based, rather than overseas, production. As global competition has accelerated, a market serving strategy has been evolving from export to international production, like the strategy adopted by Japanese firms (Tachiki, 1994). This has put pressure on Korea's export strategy, as shown by the changing position of Korean made video cassette disk players (CDPs) in China.

FIGURE 3
DESIGN CAPABILITY OF MAJOR TV BRANDS

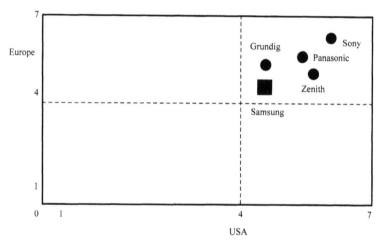

Note: 0 (low)   7 (high)

Source: Compiled from Han (1990: 228–30).

The video CDP market in China has been dominated by Korean products, competing with those imported from Japan. Consumption increased to 500,000 units in 1996, twice as high as in 1995 (*Korean Electronic Daily*, 1995). Demand for the SEC brand video CDPs imported from Korea has far exceeded supply in the Chinese market. One of the main reasons for the maintenance of its competitive advantage was price. Korean video CDPs are half the price and of similar quality to Japanese brands. More recently, however, the fast growing video CDP market in China has been joined by Japanese and European counterparts, such as Sony, JVC, Sanyo, Pioneer and Philips, whose technological capabilities – including a particularly high capability in design and product development and production systems – are far in advance of SEC's. Japanese firms, which enjoy a strong brand preference in China, have started to reduce their prices, and they will possibly produce the product in China in cooperation with their South East Asian based R&D networks. The same applies to the local Chinese manufacturers that are able to manufacture the products at a cheaper cost, though their product quality is lower than that of SEC. The above developments present new challenges to SEC's current and future competitiveness. Whether it can be maintained depends on SEC's ability to build more sophisticated technological capabilities quickly.

CONCLUSION

SEC's establishment of international production bases in China needs to be understood as a strategic move in the face of growing global competition. International production had a twofold objective: SEC wished to penetrate the local Chinese market, and serve the regional and global market from a new production base. The competitive advantage of SEC's end product subsidiaries derives from two types of inter-organizational alliance. The first is the use of intra-firm alliances. SEC's international production strategy was fairly well designed in cooperation with affiliated companies, and this was probably driven by SEC's rapid organizational reform in 1993. As a result, SEC established production networks in China quickly by transferring its technological capability in the manufacture of consumer electronics, telecommunication and semiconductor products, including standardized end product assembly and sophisticated components manufacturing technology. Hence, the China based SEC end product subsidiaries quickly linked with affiliated component manufacturing subsidiaries. SEC achieved economies of scale in local production in China within a short period of time because the majority of components were not only distributed to the local Chinese market, but also sold to their global networks.

The second form of competitive advantage is via an inter-firm alliance. SEC preferred to form JVs with experienced Chinese manufacturing firms which had a certain degree of production capability, so that the subsidiaries were easily able to upgrade their production capability. More specifically, SEC subsidiaries' competitive advantage mainly came from their production, rather than from product innovation, capability. This is classified as a temporary manifestation of the latecomer MNCs' competitive advantage. However, production capability can easily be overtaken by indigenous firms which learn and improve from the activities of MNCs. At the same time, established MNCs continued to improve their product innovation capability and SEC in turn is trying to learn and upgrade from these developments. SEC has to pit itself against two types of competitor: indigenous Chinese firms and established MNCs. There is no doubt that SEC's competitive advantage is challenged by the fast growing production capability of Chinese indigenous firms and the superior product innovation and development capability of established MNCs, given that 'competition among firms is based upon the differential capabilities, and their capabilities to expand by the creation and replication of new knowledge faster than the imitative and innovative efforts of competitors' (Kogut and Zander, 1993: 637). Ironically, the pace of improvement of SEC's foreign subsidiaries' product innovation capability seems to be diminished because of their alliance.

There are two weaknesses in SEC's interorganizational alliances. The first is the centralized interaction between headquarters and foreign subsidiaries, particularly in marketing and R&D activities, which has impeded subsidiaries from creating new capabilities essential for a quick response to a changing market environment. The second weakness is the reluctance of both JV partners to invest in the transfer of more sophisticated technological capabilities; and the speed of transfer and development of technological capabilities is slower than in wholly-owned subsidiaries. The SEC case in China suggests that strategic alliances which have been so popular amongst global players seeking complementary assets or technological capabilities may not be the best strategy to maintain a sustainable competitive advantage, unless appropriate innovation strategies are put in place.

During the home based production stage (in the 1970s–80s), SEC performed well, forming strategic alliances. SEC was mainly involved in production activities, and international marketing and product design were undertaken by the foreign distributors. Thus, SEC's competitive advantage then largely depended on its production capability. However, when production was forced to shift from the home to the foreign base in response to growing global competition, this strategic alliance faltered. When its partners' capability was no longer available, SEC's strategic weapon of production capability was also ineffective. SEC's product innovation and development capability was too weak to gain competitiveness in a marketplace where established MNCs tended to produce the same product items as SEC. Thus, SEC's competitiveness decreased drastically.

In this consideration of latecomer MNCs' foreign manufacturing subsidiaries, SEC's case raises two important issues. First, foreign subsidiaries are essential to the development of a production innovation capability that responds quickly to specific regional and local customers' preferences in the course of the transition from the global market to a local and regional market strategy. In doing so, research, design and product development must be located near to the production facilities. In order to meet the need for local and regional responsiveness, while facing growing global competition, latecomer MNCs' subsidiaries need to improve their product innovation capability, by combining knowledge transferred from headquarters and overseas design and development centres, with information and knowledge gained in the foreign market where the production plant is located. Second, short term cost minimizing through over-dependence on equity based strategic alliances without specific long term innovation strategies, be they intra-firm or inter-firm, is a risky means of sustaining competitive advantage.

ACKNOWLEDGEMENTS

The author would like to thank Dieter Ernst and David Teece (University of California, Berkeley), Sung-Tack, Park (Korea Institutue for Industrial Economics and Trade), Ken Iijima and Dennis Tachiki (Sakura Institute of Research), Ian Vertinsky (University of British Columbia), C.A. Bartlett and D.J. Collis (Harvard Business School), Mike Hobday and Keith Pavitt (University of Sussex), S.J. Nicholas (University of Melbourne), John Stopford (London Business School), John Cantwell (University of Reading), Tetsuo Abo (University of Tokyo) and Idris Sulaiman (ANU) for their helpful assistance and comments. Special thanks go to Peter Drysdale, Hal Hill and Mark Dodgson. (The Australian National University) for their guidance and kind support. I am also grateful to Tack-Myong Kim and Chang-Sik Yoon for their assitance. I am indebted to Samsung Economic Research Institute and Samsung managers with whom I interviewed in China, Korea and Southeast Asia. The views expressed, and any remaining errors, are solely my own responsibility.

NOTES

1. From now on 'Korea' is used as shorthand for South Korea.
2. The interviews were held with more than 100 managers involved in management and functional levels such as production, marketing, R&D, logistic, purchasing, finance, human resources and training. Their positions covered junior managers, section managers and executive managers. Open questions were asked according to interview questionnaires.
3. 'High' is, obviously, relative. Such costs may be high compared with some Asian economies, but not other countries. Thus, the UK is seen as a 'low' cost site within Europe.
4. However, the recent Asian financial crisis has hit Korean overseas investment, as in the UK.

REFERENCES

Archer, H.J. (1986) 'An Eclectic Approach to the Historical Study of UK Multinational Enterprises', Unpublished Ph.D. Thesis, University of Reading.

Baba, Y. and Hatashima, H. (1995) 'Capability Transfer in the Pacific Rim Nations: The Case of Japanese Electrical and Electronics Firms', *International Journal of Technology Management*, Vol. 10, Nos. 7/8, pp. 732–46.

Bartlett, C.A. (1986) *Building and Managing the Transnational: The New Organizational Challenge*. Boston, MA: Harvard Business School.

Bartlett, C.A. and Ghoshal, S. (1988) 'Managing Innovations in the Transnational Corporations', in C.A. Bartlett, Y. Doz and G. Hedlund (eds), *Research on Multinational Management*, London: Addison-Wesley.

Bloom, M. (1992) *Technological Change in the Korean Electronics Industry*. Paris: OECD.

Business Times (1994) 19 Sept.

Cantwell, J. (1991) *The Theory of Technological Competence and its Application to International Production*. Calgary, Canada: University of Calgary Press.

Choi, D.W. and Kenny, M. (1995) *The Globalisation of Korean Industry: Korean Maquiladoras in Mexico*, mimeo, University of Southern California.

Ernst, D. (1994) 'What are the Limits to the Korean Model? The Korean Electronics Industry Under Pressure', The Berkeley Roundtable on the International Economy (BRIE), University of California at Berkeley.

Han, C.M. (1990), '*Marketing Junryak*' (Marketing Strategy), in Sunwoo *et al.* (eds), *Gajun Sanupeui Kukjei Kyungjangryuk Jungdaerul Weehan Yunka* (A Study on the Increasing International Competitiveness of the Consumer Electronics Industry), Seoul, Korea Institute for Industrial Economics and Trade.

Hobday, M. (1995) 'East Asian Latecomer Firms: Learning the Technology of Electronics', *World Development*, Vol. 23, No. 7.

Hu, Y.S. (1995) 'The International Transferability of the Firm's Advantages', *California Management Review*, Vol. 37, No. 4, pp. 73–87.

Jun, Y. and Han, J.-W. (1994) *Cho-u-ryang Ki-up-euro Ka-nun-kil* (A Way towards the Best Firm). Seoul: Kimyoungsa.

Jun, Y. and Kang, S.-Y. (1994) *Samsung-junja Bumun-eui Kuk-jae Network Jun-ryak: Dongnam-a Saeng-san Network Sare* (International Networking Strategy of Samsung Electronics: A

Case of Production Networking in Southeast Asia). Seoul: Chung Ang University.

Kim, Y.H. and Campbell, N. (1994) *Strategic Control in Korean MNCs.* Working Paper No. 272, Manchester Business School.

Kim, Y. (1996) 'Technological capabilities and Samsung Electronics' International Production Network in Asia', in D. Ernst, M. Borros and S. Haggard (eds), *Asian Production Networks in Electronics: Their Impact on Trade and Technology Diffusion.* Oxford: Oxford University Press.

Kogut, B. and Zander, U. (1993) 'Knowledge of the Firm and the Evolutionary Theory of the Multinational Corporation', *Journal of International Business Studies*, Vol. 24, No. 4.

Koh, D.J. (1992) 'Beyond Technological Dependency, toward an Agile Giant: The Strategic Concerns of Korea's Samsung Electronics Co. for the 1990s', Unpublished M.Sc. Thesis, SPRU, University of Sussex.

Korean Economic Daily (1995) 3 Nov. 1995.

Korean Electronic Daily (1995) 18 Nov. 1995.

Lee, C. (1995) 'Globalisation of Korean Firm' in D.F. Simon (ed.), *Corporate Strategies in The Pacific Rim: Global versus Regional Trends.* London: Routledge, pp. 250–66.

Nikkei Industrial News (1992) 21 April.

Nikkei Industrial News (1993a) 28 July.

Nikkei Industrial News (1993b) 22 Nov.

Nikkei Industrial News (1995) 11 Jan.

Nikkei Top (1991a) 7 March.

Nikkei Top (1991b) 19 Nov.

Nikkei Top (1992a) 14 Feb.

Nikkei Top (1992b) 13 April.

Nikkei Top (1992c) 9 Dec.

Nikkei Top (1993a) 6 Oct.

Nikkei Top (1993b) 6 Dec.

Nikkei Top (1994a) 6 July.

Nikkei Top (1994b) 23 Aug.

Nikkei Top (1994c) 12 Sep.

Nikkei Top (1995a) 10 May.

Nikkei Top (1995b) 7 July.

Rowley, C. (ed.) (1998) *HRM in the Asia Pacific Region: Convergence Questioned.* London: Frank Cass.

Samsung (1993) *Samsung Sin-kyung-yeong: Na-bu-teo Byun-haiya-handa* (The New Management of Samsung: Get Myself Changed). Seoul: Samsung Group.

SEC (Samsung Electronics Co. Ltd) (1989) *Samsung Junja 20-nyun-sa* (The 25 Year History of Samsung Electronics). Seoul.

SEC (Samsung Electronics Co. Ltd) (1995a) *Guide to Out Bound Presentation Kit.* Global Operations Division.

SEC (Samsung Electronics Co. Ltd) (1995b) Samsung Electronics in Brief.

SEM (*Samsung Jun-ki Sa-bo*, Samsung Electro-Mechanics' Monthly Magazine) (1994) Jan–Dec.

SEMM (*Samsung Jun-ja Sa-bo*, Samsung Electronics' Monthly Magazine), Jan. 1990 to Dec. 1994.

SED (Samsung Electron-Devices Co. Ltd) (1990) *Samsung Jun-kwan 20-nyun-sa* (The 20 Year History of Samsung Electron-Devices). Seoul.

SC (Samsung Corning Co. Ltd) (1994) *Samsung Corning 20-nyun-sa* (The 20 Year History of Samsung Corning). Seoul.

SMM (*Samsung Sa-bo*, Samsung Monthly Magazine), Jan. 1980 to Dec. 1994.

Tachiki, D. (1995) 'Corporate Investment Strategies for the Pacific Region: Some Evolving Changes in Japanese FDI', Presented to the Center on Japanese Economy and Business, Columbia University.

Tsuda, M. and Shinada, N. (1995) 'Problems concerning the International Competitiveness of the Electronics and Electric Machinery Industry', *Japan Development Bank*, No. 46.

Wall Street Journal (1994) 4 March.

World Bank (1990), *China Electronics Sector Report*, Report No. 7962-CHA, Industry and Energy Operations Division, China Department, Asia region, World Bank.

Wyatt, S.M.E., Bertin, G. and Pavitt, K. (1985) 'Patents and Multinational Corporations: Results from Questionnaires', *World Patent Information*, 7, pp. 196–212.

The Emergence of Korean and Taiwanese Multinationals in Europe: Prospects and Limitations

ROGER VAN HOESEL

For a long time, the promotion of manufactured exports has been regarded as the most important engine of the South Korean[1] and Taiwanese economies. At present, however, their crossborder business activities are no longer merely confined to exports. Since the end of the 1970s, Korean and Taiwanese companies have also started to invest abroad. Although early investments from (by that time) developing countries received considerable academic attention,[2] much less is known about more recent Korean and Taiwanese foreign direct investment (FDI) (cf. Ki, 1992; van Hoesel, 1992, 1996; Dunning *et al.*, 1997). This holds especially for their operations in Europe, which have hardly been studied (McDermott and Young, 1989; McDermott, 1991; Probert, 1991). In this contribution, the case study method is used to gain a deeper insight into the typical features of the internationalization patterns of Korean and Taiwanese companies and the problems they face in operating in Europe. On the basis of this analysis, tentative conclusions will be drawn about the prospects and limitations of Korean and Taiwanese investment in Europe. A basic proposition here is that Korean and Taiwanese companies cannot simply be equated with 'conventional' American or European multinational companies (MNCs). It is argued here that the so-called 'late industrialization' pattern of the Korean and Taiwanese economies may have important implications for the internationalization of their leading companies. Before discussing the theoretical arguments on which this proposition is based, a brief empirical overview of Korean and Taiwanese outward investment is given.

KOREA AND TAIWAN AS OUTWARD INVESTORS

Until the mid-1980s, Korean and Taiwanese overseas investment projects were usually limited in size and for the most part confined to their own, Asian, region. Since the second half of the 1980s, however, the size of outward investment has increased quite rapidly, making Korea and Taiwan among the most important new home countries of MNCs (cf. Dunning *et al.*, 1997). In the case of Korea, only in 1987 did FDI flows for the first time exceed US$ 100 million. Since then, the size of annual FDI increased every year. Since 1991, annual Korean outward direct investment amounted to

Roger van Hoesel, Buck Consultants International, The Netherlands more than US$ 1 billion, reaching US$ 3.1 billion in 1995. For Taiwan, a similar rapid growth of outward investment can be observed. The emergence of Taiwanese investors abroad also assumed substantial proportions from 1987 onwards. The approved annual FDI went up from US$ 103 million in 1987 to US$ 2.5 billion in 1995.

Not only has the size of Korean and Taiwanese FDI increased considerably in recent years, it has also become less of a regional phenomenon. Table 1 presents the geographical distribution of Korean and Taiwanese outward FDI stock in 1978 and 1995. It illustrates that companies from both economies have found their way to industrialized economies. Although the US, historically a major partner of Korea and Taiwan, had attracted most FDI in the industrialized world, the importance of Europe as a host region is also clearly on the rise – certainly in the case of Korea.

TABLE 1
GEOGRAPHICAL DISTRIBUTION OF OUTWARD FDI STOCK: KOREA AND TAIWAN

	1978 Korea (%)	Taiwan (%)	1995 Korea (%)	Taiwan (%)
Asia	52.5	70.8	44.7	61.1
Europe	2.8	0.3	15.1	3.5
North America	18.7	16.5	30.8	17.4
Latin America	1.8	7.4	3.3	17.0
Oceania	2.6	4.2	2.4	0.4
Other areas	21.6	0.8	3.7	0.6
Total ($US m)	71.6	49.9	10,224	15,899

Sources: Bank of Korea; Ministry of Economic Affairs (ROC).

This rapid expansion of Korean and Taiwanese presence abroad was caused by a multitude of factors. First of all, the fast growth of FDI flows would not have been possible without a major change in government policy with regard to outward investment (UNCTAD, 1995). For a long time this policy mainly consisted of capital export restrictions to keep investments at home. This attitude changed in the second half of the 1980s when Korea and Taiwan were confronted with a rapid erosion of traditional comparative advantages. A shortage of low skilled labour had started to push industrial wages up, a trend that was reinforced by democratization tendencies that gave more room for wage demands by labour unions.[3] These wage increases were not matched by productivity growth. As a consequence, companies started to shift the more labour intensive production activities to cheaper labour cost, often neighbouring, countries. The gradual industrial upgrading of the economies had also led to more intense direct competition with producers from major trading partners. As a response to their export successes, the US authorities (for Korea and Taiwan the most important markets) forced the Korean Won and New Taiwan dollar to appreciate considerably *vis-à-vis* the US dollar.[4] This clearly made exporting from the home economies less attractive. An important reason why especially Korean companies have started to invest on such a large scale in Europe were the protectionist measures against their products. Other motivations as to why the companies decided to establish production in Europe will be discussed in more detail in the case studies.

THEORETICAL FRAME OF REFERENCE: LATE INDUSTRIALIZATION AND OUTWARD DIRECT INVESTMENT

Countries that industrialized only this century share several characteristics that are eloquently voiced by the 'Late Industrialization' (LI) paradigm (cf. Amsden 1989, 1991; Amsden and Hikino, 1993; Hikino and Amsden, 1994). According to this concept, in late industrialized economies (LIEs) 'learning from others' (or 'borrowing' technology) was initially the most important input for their technological enhancement – as opposed to economies that emerged during the First (Britain, end of the eighteenth century) and the Second (especially Germany and the US, about 100 years later) Industrial Revolutions. In the latter countries, inventions and innovations were the major forces behind industrialization. The LI paradigm argues that this divergent starting point has influenced the industrialization of countries such as Korea and Taiwan in various ways.

First, governments in these countries have played an active – and often dominant – role in overcoming the fundamental handicaps that local companies faced. Not only did even leading firms lack substantial firm specific advantages, but also technological leap-frogging has not often been a realistic option. Leading enterprises from the US, Japan and Europe (the 'Triad') increasingly erected entry barriers around their proprietary technology, which keeps newcomers out – at least for frontier technologies (Hikino and Amsden, 1994). In addition, the low wage comparative advantage has proved to be only temporary in nature. Hikino and Amsden (1994) argue that, as a result, successful late industrialization requires, among other things, subsidizing production costs (such as capital) to 'get the prices wrong' (as opposed to 'getting the prices right').

A second characteristic of late industrializers concerns the typical use of 'mid-technologies' by leading firms. Focusing on the bottom of the market would mean tough competition from low wage countries while higher technologies are made impenetrable by innovating companies from the Triad. To gain a competitive edge (also *vis-à-vis* 'mature' Triad companies in the market), LIE companies had to focus on their shopfloor operations. Achieving small, incremental improvements in productivity – resulting in low costs and improved price competitiveness – and product quality have been crucial.[5]

A third feature of late industrialization concerns the structure of leading companies. In many branches of industry there has been a continuous risk that mid-technology products become obsolete because of the introduction of a revolutionary new product. We often observe the emergence of conglomerates in LIEs that, to reduce this risk, typically operate in technologically rather unrelated industries. Examples are the Korean companies that will be discussed in the next section. The size of these companies puts them in a better position to seize the funds required to invest in foreign technology, hire highly qualified engineers and managers or expand production capacity.

The LI paradigm basically provides a broad historical explanation of how countries have been able to industrialize in recent periods. What is lacking in the original analysis, however, is a further distinction between research and development (R&D) (or innovational), production and marketing capabilities of leading companies. This nuance is especially important for understanding the internationalization pattern of the companies involved. In addition to superior technological (R&D) know-how, leading enterprises from *early* industrialized countries for a long time have also possessed – to a greater or less extent – a 'marketing monopoly' in many industries. Figure 1 illustrates in a simplified manner how the strategic focus of leading companies from these early industrialized economies has evolved over time.

FIGURE 1
STRATEGIC FOCI OF LEADING COMPANIES FROM EARLY INDUSTRIALISED
ECONOMIES (NOT DRAWN TO SCALE)

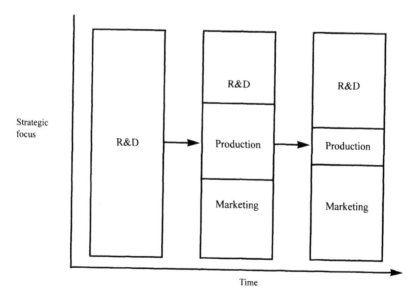

As is argued by the LI paradigm, in leading companies from early industrialized nations inventions or innovations – resulting from R&D efforts – usually precede commercial production. After the product is introduced in a market, marketing usually becomes more important. The emergence of new competitors forced firms to develop marketing strengths (such as promotional skills and extensive distribution channels) to maintain or expand their market share. In a continuous effort to keep up with other inventing or innovating companies, R&D remains a relatively important function. In time, as shown in Figure 1, production itself becomes less of a strategic focus. One of the reasons for this shift in strategic foci is the international distribution of operations that has emerged since the 1960s, in which leading companies from early industrialized countries increasingly began to subcontract the first part of their production process (*viz.* intermediate goods) and later on also the production of final goods (original equipment manufacturing or OEM) to indigenous companies in LIEs. We saw that, according to the LI paradigm, in the latter economies the strategic focus historically has always been on their shopfloor operations. This has led to the situation that, although substantial export volumes were realized through OEM sales, for these LIE firms there was no need and/or basis to internationalize further by means of FDI. Only recently have marketing as well as R&D gained some importance. Figure 2 illustrates this shift in the relative importance of their strategic foci.

FIGURE 2
STRATEGIC FOCI OF LEADING COMPANIES FROM LIEs
(NOT DRAWN TO SCALE)

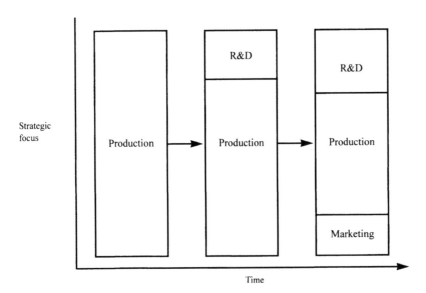

There are a priori reasons to assume that this industrialization path influences the internationalization of their companies. According to the LI paradigm, leading companies from these economies do not have the typical assets (such as innovational and marketing strengths) needed to invest abroad – certainly not in greenfield ventures in economically advanced economies.[6] Also, according to conventional MNC theory (cf. Dunning,

1988, 1993), such firm-specific advantages are needed to produce outside a home country. Nevertheless, we have observed that FDI from Korea and Taiwan – also in the industrialized world – is clearly on the rise. To what extent does their development path hinder their (further) global presence, in Europe? To gain a deeper understanding of this phenomenon, the investments by a limited number of Korean and Taiwanese companies will be investigated in more detail.

INVESTING IN EUROPE: FOUR CASE STUDIES

The cases of the two leading companies in Korea's consumer electronics industry (Samsung Electronics, LG Electronics) and two in Taiwan's computer industry (ACER, First International Computer) are discussed here. These branches of industry were chosen because they have reached a relatively high degree of internationalization (in terms of FDI) in their respective home economies. In each case, specific attention is paid to the actual operations in Europe, the motivations to invest and the difficulties faced in operating there. The information reflected in the cases is based on in-depth interviews with executives at the central and the regional headquarters as well as information (secondary) provided by the companies. Added to this material was information gathered from publications in other sources (external).

Korean Consumer Electronics

Although the consumer electronics (CE) industry in Korea emerged only three and a half decades ago,[7] its achievements by all standards are impressive (Bloom, 1991, 1992). At present, the size of the Korean CE industry is second in the world after Japan. The domestic industry has a highly oligopolistic structure that is dominated by only three companies – Samsung Electronics and LG Electronics, the two biggest, and Daewoo Electronics.

Samsung Electronics

Samsung Electronics Co. (SEC) was founded in 1969 as part of the Samsung Group, one of Korea's oldest and largest conglomerates.[8] In 1972, the company started to produce black and white televisions (TVs). Since then, the product line has been extended substantially. The size of SEC has grown accordingly. Between 1985 and 1994, for instance, total sales grew from US$ 1.5 billion to US$ 14.6 billion. At present, SEC is involved in a wide range of activities covering CE, semiconductors, computers and information systems.

The establishment of a colour TV (CTV) factory in Portugal in 1982 was the first production facility established by SEC outside Korea (though this factory is no longer in operation). By 1994, SEC had built up an impressive presence in Europe, where 21 per cent of total sales was realized (see Table 2). At present, SEC has invested in six production facilities in Europe.

CTVs are produced in plants in the UK (established in 1987), and in Hungary (established in 1989). Spain was selected in 1989 to produce video cassette recorders (VCRs). In the Slovak Republic, SEC in 1991 formed a joint venture (JV) with Caltex (44.8 per cent owned by SEC) to produce refrigerators. In the same year, SEC, together with Texas Instruments (TI) of the US, invested in a factory in Portugal (38 per cent owned by SEC) to produce memory chips for the European market. In Turkey, SEC has a 20 per cent stake in a CTV plant. Next to these factories, SEC has established sales offices in Germany, the UK, France, Spain, Italy, Sweden and Portugal. In the UK, a small R&D centre undertakes work on telecommunication systems, audiovisual systems and home appliances. The centre primarily focuses on local market developments; more fundamental research takes place in Korea.

TABLE 2
SEC'S MAJOR OPERATIONS IN EUROPE: SOME FACTUAL DATA (SPRING 1995)

Country	Year of establish-ment	Activities	Employees (full time)	Korean employees	Annual produc-tion capacity (units)
Portugal	1994	P, SE**	165	8	4 Mbit DRAM 1 m
UK*	1987	P, SE	425	7	16 Mbit DRAM 0.3m
Spain	1989	P, SE	210	5	CTV 700k
Slovakia	1991	P, SE***	942	5	VCR 700k
Hungary	1989	P, SE	201	6	REF 360k
Turkey	1989	P, SE	310		CTV 120k
Germany	1982	HQ, W	112	12	CTV 200k
UK	1984	S	124	9	nr
France	1988	W, S	81	6	nr
Spain	1990	W, S	67	6	nr
Italy	1991	W, S	36	5	nr
Sweden	1992	W, S	21	4	nr
Portugal	1993	W, S	30	2	nr

Key:
* = Wynyard facility is not yet included
** = 38% ownership; JV with Texas instruments
*** = 44.8% ownership, JV with Caltex
P = production
SE = service
HQ = headquarters
W = warehousing
S = sales
REF = refrigerators
nr = not relevant

Source: SEC.

Until the beginning of the 1990s, fear of protectionist measures was the prime motivation to shift part of production to Europe – a fear that was not unjustified. In an attempt to protect its own CE industry (Philips, Grundig), the European Union (EU) has frequently threatened, and occasionally utilized, various protectionist instruments to discourage the consumption of (imported) Korean CE products. The decision to produce locally was, however, not merely based on defensive considerations. Another – although less important – reason to invest in Europe has been to gather marketing information to support exports to the continent. An example of the latter is the 'Euro-lab' in Frankfurt where, among other things, European food habits are investigated – information that is used to adapt existing products or develop new ones. In the 1990s we can observe a shift towards a more offensive attitude to expand production operations in (Western) Europe. With stricter local content requirements in place,[9] SEC decided to gradually further localize its European operations. The acquisition in 1994 of the TV glass bulb manufacturer FGT (located in former East Germany) by its sister company Samsung Corning is an example of SEC's attempts to transform its production operations from screwdriver plants into truly localized manufacturing operations.

We asked senior executives at the company's headquarters as well as at the regional head office to express their assessment of the *perceived* strengths and weaknesses of SEC *vis-à-vis* its competitors in the Korean and EU markets with regard to CE products (see Table 3). Although this merely represents a personal judgement of the interviewees, it nevertheless reveals a number of interesting insights. With regard to technological capabilities, patents, cost structure and product quality, no, or only a small, deviation exists between the perceived positions in Korea and Europe. This appears to confirm the conventional strength in shopfloor operations of companies originating in LIEs. Also, with regard to the quality and attitude of its workforce, access to capital, and managerial capabilities, no major differences appear to exist between the home market and Europe.

This, however, is where the similarities come to an end. In view of the company's goal to localize production, its present capacity in Europe is still insufficient. This is also underlined by SEC's decision to invest heavily in new production facilities in the UK.[10] More striking is the perceived relatively weak position in Europe in terms of the company's marketing capabilities. With regard to all the items listed related to marketing (breadth of product line, brand names, distribution, advertising/promotion skills, sales force, service, knowledge of customers' needs and loyalty of customers), the company perceives its position as (considerably) weaker in Western Europe than in Korea. The biggest difference exists with regard to brand awareness, which is considered to be relatively weak in Europe, whereas in Korea the Samsung brand name is very well established. The company is of the opinion that it is impossible to aim at becoming a global leader in electronics and, at the same time, remain dependent on OEM contracts.[11] In the past, OEM business has been by far the most important way to sell products in Europe. In other words, although SEC did sell substantial volumes in the European market, most of it was sold under the label of other companies. SEC in 1993 introduced a three-year programme to convert the company in Europe from a production orientated into a marketing oriented enterprise. This not only implied that substantial amounts had to be allocated to promotion activities, but also had important

TABLE 3
STRENGTHS AND WEAKNESSES IN CE PRODUCTS

	SEC		LGE	
	Korea	Europe	Korea	Europe
Technological capability	3	2	3	0
Patents	3	2	3	0
Cost structure	2	3	2	2
Workforce and attitude	3	2–3	3	1
Production capacity	3	1	3	3
Access to capital	2	3	3	2
Managerial capability	2	2	3	0
Product quality	2	2	3	1
Product differentiation	2	1	3	0
Brand names	2	-1	3	-1
Distribution channels	2	0	2	1
Advertising/promotion skills	2	0	2	0
Sales force	2	1	2	0
Service	3	1–2	2	-1
Knowledge of customers' needs	2	0	3	-1
Loyalty of customers	2	0	3	-2

Key:
-3 = very weak position
-2 = weak position
-1 = relatively weak position
0 = neutral
+1 = relatively strong position
+2 = strong position
+3 = very strong position

Sources: Interviews held at parent companies and European headquarters.

consequences for the organization as a whole. A direct result has been the decision to substantially expand the distribution network in Europe.[12] A more indirect implication of the programme is the greater autonomy of the West European operations. In addition, SEC has committed itself to hire more local personnel in managerial positions. Two years after the introduction of this new strategic direction, the first results are visible. In relatively 'easy' markets, such as the Czech and Slovak Republics, Hungary and Romania, SEC has performed very well. In large markets, such as Germany and France, SEC has not yet been able to capture substantial market shares for its Samsung brand products, though recently important progress has also been made there.

LG (Lucky-Goldstar) Electronics

LG Electronics (LGE), formerly known as Goldstar Co., was founded in 1958 as the first indigenous electronics manufacturer in Korea.[13] LGE often acted as a pioneer in the Korean electronics business: for instance, in 1959 the company was the first in Korea to produce a transistor radio. Likewise, Goldstar established the first private R&D facility in Korea in 1975. As in the case of SEC, LGE has experienced rapid growth. Total sales, for example, increased almost fivefold between 1985 and 1994, from US$ 1.4

billion to US$ 6.5 billion. Compared to the product line of SEC, CE represent a much more sizeable part of LGE's total sales. Semiconductors, in the case of SEC the most important product category, are produced by other members of the LG Group. For LGE, home appliances, audio and video equipment, CTVs, and computer and office equipment are the most important products.

In 1994, LGE realized 19 per cent of its total sales in Europe. Although not as extensive as SEC, LGE also has built up a substantial physical presence on the continent (see Table 4). In 1986, LGE invested in its first production facility in Europe, a CTV factory in Germany. By 1995, LGE had three manufacturing facilities in Europe, four sales subsidiaries, and a research centre. In the beginning of 1995, the factory in Germany produced CTVs and VCRs; in the near future CTV production will be moved to the UK to be integrated with existing operations there. The original plant in the UK, established in 1988, produces microwave ovens and CTVs. In the Italian plant, set up in 1990, refrigerators are produced.[14] Next to the factories LGE operates sales subsidiaries in the UK, France, Germany and Hungary. At LG Design Technology in Dublin, Ireland, products are designed that are tailored to European lifestyles and local consumers. LGE's commitment to gain a stronger position in the European market is also illustrated by a permanent exposition hall that was opened in 1992 in Prague (the first established by Korean appliance makers in Europe), where it exclusively exhibits its home appliances.

LGEs' motivations to invest in the EU are similar to SEC's. Initially, a

TABLE 4
LGE'S MAJOR OPERATIONS IN EUROPE: SOME FACTUAL DATA (SPRING 1995)

Country	Year of establishment	Activities	Employees (full time)	Annual production capacity (units)
Germany	1986	P	282	CTV 300k, VCR 700k
UK	1988	P	334	MO 700k, CTV 200k
Italy	1990	P	180	REF 200k
Ireland	1992	D	7	nr
Germany	1980	HQ, W, S, SE	70	nr
France	1990	W, S, SE	40	nr
UK	1987	W, S, SE	52	nr
Hungary	1992	S, W, SE	10	nr

Key:
P = production
D = design
HQ = headquarters
W = warehousing
S = sales
SE = service
MO = microwave ovens
REF = refrigerators
nr = not relevant

Source: LGE.

major reason to shift production was the company's fear of protectionist measures. LGE (as well as SEC) among others was hit several times by anti-dumping measures. As a result of stricter local content requirements, the initial response to assemble imported inputs locally has become less adequate. In this light, the company's wish to localize its overseas operations, as voiced in the 1990s, is not surprising. However, in contrast to SEC, LGE apparently has not yet taken concrete measures to speed up local vertical integration. Another very important reason to have a physical presence in Europe is that this enables the company to gather information about market trends and local consumer preferences. The design centre in Ireland was specifically established for that purpose.

What are the perceived strengths and weaknesses in Korea and Western Europe with regard to CE products, according to senior executives in Korea and Europe? We can see these in Table 3. Except for two items (production capacity and cost structure), LGE perceives its position as weaker in Europe than in the home market. With regard to technological capabilities and patents, the company takes a neutral position in Europe, whereas in Korea its position was labelled as 'very strong'. Also, the scores with regard to 'workforce and their attitude' and 'product quality' are considerably lower in Europe than in Korea. Interestingly, and in contrast to SEC's, LGE's production capacity in Europe is not considered a problem; this notion is confirmed by the fact that the German factory, for example, in 1995 had excess production capacity.[15]

As in the case of SEC, Table 3 clearly illustrates the company's relative weakness in terms of marketing capabilities. With respect to all relevant items mentioned, LGE considers its position in Western Europe to be weaker than in Korea. With regard to brand names, service rendered and knowledge of customers' needs, LGE perceives its position in Europe as 'relatively weak', whereas the loyalty of customers with regard to LGE's products was even labelled as 'weak'. According to one interviewee,[16] customers in Germany, for instance, perceive LGE's products as 'third rate' (with local products and Japanese being first and second rate, respectively), being low priced but also of low quality. LGE perceives companies like SEC and Japanese Panasonic as its major competitors. According to LGE, the company does not directly compete with top brands such as Sony and Philips. The company does not invest as much as SEC in the improvement of its marketing performance in Europe. A continued focus on the production side of operations and a relative ignorance of the marketing function may force the company to maintain its low price strategy. In Western Europe, OEM sales remain relatively important and are seen as a means to utilize existing excess capacity. Until now, LGE has not yet been able to break out of this deadlock. The shift of CTV production from Germany to a new plant in the UK is expected to further lower production costs. An additional difficulty appears to be the critical attitude of European consumers regarding Korean product designs. LGE pays substantial attention to this problem. Next to the Design Centre, this is also illustrated by LGEs' sponsoring of an exhibition at the Royal College of Art in London, which is well known for the high level of designers trained at the institute (*Financial Times*, 1995). As in the case of SEC, the relatively weak position of LGE does not hold for its operations in Eastern Europe. Here, where the company only sells under its own brand name, LGE has acquired a relatively strong position for some products.

Taiwanese Computer Industry

In less than a decade and a half the computer industry in Taiwan has developed into one of its most successful branches of industry (van Hoesel, 1996). Also, internationally its position has improved very rapidly. In 1985 Taiwan was the thirteenth ranked producer of information products in the world; by 1993, it occupied the fifth position. In some fields, especially those related to personal computer (PC) and notebook systems, Taiwan has even become one of the global leaders.[17] In contrast to the Korean CE industry, the computer industry in Taiwan is highly competitive, with hundreds of suppliers for some products and markets that are open to foreign companies. In 1994, ACER and First International Computer (FIC) were the two biggest computer producers in Taiwan.

ACER

ACER, initially named Multitech, was founded in 1976 with capital of only US$ 25,000 and 11 employees. ACER has become Taiwan's most successful computer company, widely accepted as an example for other local computer companies to follow. After having started as a service company and representative for overseas companies, in 1981 the first computers were produced. Between 1988 and 1994, total sales grew from US$ 531 million to US$ 3.2 billion. ACER's most important product categories are PC systems, notebooks, and peripherals. To minimize its dependency on external suppliers, it increasingly invests in the production of components such as memory chips and ASICs.

ACER realizes about 20 per cent of its total turnover in Europe. During the last few years, the company has extended its presence in Europe considerably. At present, it operates three assembly lines on the continent (see Table 5). Although the company established its first sales office in Europe as early as in 1985, only in 1992, 1993 and 1994 did assembly begin in The Netherlands, Germany and the UK, respectively. In The Netherlands and Germany, both PC systems and notebooks are produced, whereas in the UK, only PC systems are assembled. Next to these assembly lines ACER established sales offices in France, the UK, Italy, Austria, Belgium, Denmark, Norway, Spain and Hungary. Notwithstanding the large number of local ventures, it should be stressed that, as a whole, ACER's operations in Europe are relatively small scale compared to those of SEC and LGE. In 1994, ACER in total employed about 360 in Europe whereas LGE and SEC had approximately 965 and 3,300 employees respectively.

TABLE 5
ACER'S OPERATIONS IN EUROPE – SOME FACTUAL DATA (SPRING 1995)

Country	Year of establishment	Activities	Employees (full time)	Annual production capacity (units)
Netherlands	1990/92	P, W, S, SE, HQ	110	PCs 180k
Germany	1985/93	P, W, S, SE	120	PCs 120k
France	1988	W, S, SE	26	nr
UK	1988/94	P, W, S, SE	43	PCs 60k
Italy	1990	W, S, SE	15	nr
Austria	1992	W, S, SE	16	nr
Belgium	1993	S, SE	6	nr
Denmark	1990	S, SE	15	nr
Norway	1994	S, SE	3–4	nr
Spain	1995	S, SE	1–2	nr
Hungary	1994	S, SE	3	nr

Key:
P = production
W = warehousing
S = sales
SE = service
HQ = headquarters
nr = not relevant

Source: ACER.

In contrast to Korean CE companies, protectionist measures taken by the EU are no threat to Taiwanese computer sales. The importance of European competitors is too limited to justify a protectionist policy by the EU authorities.[18] For ACER, a major motivation has been the establishment of a physical presence near customers in a market that is characterized by rapidly changing demands. In this way, demands for continuously changing computer configurations can be monitored adequately and ACER's product range is modified accordingly. It simply takes too long to send finished PC or notebook systems to Europe and subsequently distribute them to the various countries. In practice, this implies that the company flies in fast moving components (such as processors), but ships other parts (such as computer cases) to Europe. These parts are then assembled into final products. As a result of this strategy, inventories are kept at a minimum. The reason for having three instead of one assembly line is that Europe (notwithstanding its unification programme) is considered to consist of separate markets, each with its own specific demands.

ACER's chairman, Stan Shih, often compares the company's strategy with the ancient game of 'Go', in which a master player will methodologically surround his opponents before moving in for the kill. Analogous to the game, patience, endurance and strategic planning are needed to win market share. In view of ACER's aspirations to become a global leader in the computer business, its present position in Europe is not yet satisfactory. Again, we asked senior executives at the Taipei headquarters and the regional headquarters in The Netherlands about the

TABLE 6
STRENGTHS AND WEAKNESSES IN PC SYSTEMS

| | ACER | | FIC | |
	Taiwan	Europe	Taiwan	Europe
Technological capability	3	3	2	1
Patents	3	0	0	0
Cost structure	0	1	2	2
Workforce and attitude	3	1	2	2
Production capacity	3	2	2	1
Access to capital	3	2	3	1
Managerial capability	3	1	0	2
Product quality	3	3	1	1
Product differentiation	3	3	0	2
Brand names	3	1	2	0
Distribution channels	3	1	2	1
Advertising/promotion skills	3	1	1	1
Sales force	3	1	1	0
Service	3	1	1	2
Knowledge of customers' needs	3	1	0	1
Loyalty of customers	3	1	0	2

Key:
-3 = very weak position
-2 = weak position
-1 = relatively weak position
0 = neutral
+1 = relatively strong position
+2 = strong position
+3 = very strong position

Sources: Interviews held at parent company and European headquarters.

perceived relative strengths and weaknesses with regard to the position of
ACER PCs in Taiwan and in Europe *vis-à-vis* its main competitors (see
Table 6). It is obvious that ACER is quite confident about the quality and
differentiation of its product line – both at home and abroad. A large gap,
however, exists with regard to the marketing achievements of its business in
Taiwan and Europe. On all the marketing aspects listed (brand name,
distribution channels, advertising and promotion skills, sales force, service
rendered, knowledge of customer's needs and the loyalty of customers),
ACER perceives its position in Europe as substantially weaker than in
Taiwan. In most countries, brand awareness, for instance, is still too low.
Since the costs involved in building up brand awareness and a positive
image are very high, this is considered a long term process in which per
country attempts are made to increase the awareness of the ACER brand.
Or, as Shih puts it, 'it takes perhaps two years to see returns from
manufacturing. Technology development may take three to four years and
require ten times as much effort. Image building takes one hundred times
the effort. It takes a very long time' (*Financial Times*, 1993). From the
beginning, ACER sold PCs under its own brand name in Taiwan and also,
later on, in the Asian region. In industrialized economies, however, the

company primarily sold through OEM buyers. An attempt by the end of the 1980s to sell only under the ACER name failed. At present, gaining OEM contracts is considered very important again, especially as a means to realize scale advantages. Nevertheless, building up a strong global brand name is still a major goal. The quality of the promotion efforts in Europe is improved by hiring local commercial and creative employees. In addition, ACER continually tries to increase the number of retailers selling its computers on the continent. Another weakness, when compared to the situation in Taiwan, is the attitude of the workforce, and, related to that, the quality of management. Moreover, the lack of labour market flexibility in much of Western Europe (for example, it is much more hazardous to fire employees than in Taiwan) is considered a serious problem. In addition, according to ACER, hiring talented young employees is not an easy task because the most promising graduates often prefer to work for better known companies. In Taiwan, ACER has at its disposal a large pool of bright university graduates who are eager to work for the company.

First International

At the beginning of the 1980s, FIC started as an automation department within the Formosa Plastics Group (FGP), one of Taiwan's largest industrial conglomerates. In 1983, for the first time PC systems were assembled – initially for internal use only. From 1986 onwards, FIC began to sell computers externally. In 1987 the company took the strategic decision to move into the production of motherboards and add-on cards. In that period FIC also entered the international market. At present FIC is one of the largest motherboard manufacturers in the world. The company has grown at a very rapid pace: its total sales went from US$ 90 million in 1990 to approximately US$ 600 million in 1994. In addition to the production of motherboards, PC systems and add-on cards, in 1994 FIC also began producing notebook systems.

For FIC, Europe is by far the most important market (representing more than half of total revenues). In contrast to most other Taiwanese computer companies who – at least initially – primarily focused on the US market, FIC first targeted the European market. As we can see from Table 7, in 1993 FIC established an assembly line in The Netherlands where PC systems, as well as notebooks, are assembled. In 1995 the company moved to a much bigger plot of land that can cater for possible production increases in the future. In addition, FIC established a European service centre in The Netherlands. Moreover, the company set up sales offices in Spain, the Czech Republic and France. Although FIC's local operations grew very rapidly (total turnover of FIC Europe grew from US$ 6 million in 1991 to US$ 55 million in 1994; this does not include OEM sales dealt with by the Taipei headquarters), it only employs in total about 70 in Europe. This is very modest if compared with SEC and LGE and even in comparison with ACER. In view of the relatively short international experience of the company and the fact that the emphasis is more on the sale of components

(motherboards and add-on cards) than that of final products (PC systems
and notebooks), it is no surprise that FIC's presence in Europe is less
extensive than ACER's.

TABLE 7
FIC'S OPERATIONS IN EUROPE: SOME FACTUAL DATA (SPRING 1995)

	Netherlands	Spain	Czech Republic	France
Year of establishment	1990	1990	1992	1994
Activities	P, W, S, SE, HQ	W, S	W, S, SE	W, S, SE
Employees (full time)	55	6	9	3
Annual production capacity (units)	PCs 60k	nr	nr	nr

Key:
P = production
W = warehousing
S = sales
SE = service
HQ = headquarters
nr = not relevant

Source: FIC.

Also, in the case of FIC, fear of protectionist measures taken by the EU
has not influenced the decision to assemble PCs and notebooks in The
Netherlands. Again, 'being close to the market' is considered to be of high
importance. However, this does not only hold for the marketing of final PCs
and notebooks: it should be realized that motherboards are usually designed
in close cooperation with the (European) buyers, which makes being close
to (potential) customers attractive for this purpose too.

We also asked FIC executives to express their opinions on the relative
strengths and weaknesses with regard to the position of FIC PC systems in
Taiwan and in Europe *vis-à-vis* its main competitors. Although not as
obvious as in the other cases, differences again occurred between the
company's position in both markets. Technological capability is rated as
much stronger in Taiwan than in Europe. As could be expected, the same
holds for production capacity, as well as access to capital. As in the case of
ACER, the brand name (LEO) and the distribution channels are considered
stronger in Taiwan than in Europe. In Taiwan and some other neighbouring
countries, LEO is a well established brand name. In the present situation,
FIC considers that the tremendous commercial and financial efforts needed
to build up own brand names and distribution channels in highly
competitive markets outside the region are not worth the risk. Another
motivation to focus on the production of intermediate products, instead of
on final products, is that too much emphasis on the marketing of its own
PCs and notebook systems could deter its buyers of motherboards who may
not be inclined to (indirectly) support one of its competitors. Disadvantages
of slim profit margins, characteristic for OEM business, are compensated
for by the large volumes produced by FIC. In addition, OEM business for

FIC means long term contracts that are highly important in a dynamic market like the computer industry. As long as FIC's major emphasis remains on the production of motherboards and on acting as an OEM supplier of PC systems and notebooks, this position is not likely to change. Noteworthy are the relatively stronger perceived managerial capabilities in Europe than in Taiwan, the better knowledge of customers' needs, and the higher degree of loyalty in Europe. The last factor most probably holds primarily for its OEM customers. The perceived strong position in service can be explained by the large service centre that FIC runs at its European headquarters.

DISCUSSION

We have shed some light on the underexposed phenomenon of Korean and Taiwanese FDI in Europe. We observed that Korean companies as a whole have invested on a considerably larger scale in Europe than their Taiwanese counterparts. This also holds for the companies studied here: SEC and LGE have built up a much larger presence in Europe than ACER, and certainly in comparison with FIC.

As far as the motivations to invest in Europe are concerned, important differences exist between the Koreans and the Taiwanese. In the case of Korean CE firms, initially the decision to shift production to inside the walls of 'Fortress Europe' was primarily a defensive act. Protectionist measures have led to an early decision to move production abroad by LGE as well as SEC – early in terms of their technological and marketing development at that time. Their desire to acquire a larger share of the European market through products sold under their own brand names in more recent years meant that collecting market information has become an additional important motivation. The recent investments by the Taiwanese companies ACER and FIC in Europe are more offensive in nature. In their case, a major reason to assemble locally has been that this enables them to respond more adequately to changing market demands and to adapt their product lines accordingly. In other words, the dynamic nature of the computer industry more or less forced these companies to localize their assembly operations.

A comparison between the case studies reveals that important similarities exist with regard to the problems they face in building up a strong position in the European market. Not only technological, but especially marketing weaknesses vis-à-vis leading companies from early industrialized economies in the CE and computer industry are major obstacles that have to be overcome. Interestingly, the strategies pursued to improve their market positions in Europe differ substantially. We noted, for instance, that the production operations (also in terms of 'local content') of SEC in Europe are more comprehensive than those of LGE. Also, in terms of marketing activities SEC is more aggressive than LGE. An important explanation for this divergence in strategy of the two companies (typically known for their 'follower strategies') is the budgets available for this complex task. Building up an own brand name and extensive distribution channels, especially in industrialized economies, requires massive financial funds. SEC has generated substantial internal financial means through its semiconductor business which – until recently – was highly profitable. As we saw earlier, the semiconductor business is not dealt with by LGE. In addition, the decision to invest heavily in industrialized economies partly seems to be a matter of a company's belief in its own capabilities and management's attitudes towards risks.

In the case of Taiwan, the differences in strategy are even more pronounced. ACER invested substantial resources to establish a sound market position in Europe. As the company lacks the scale and financial means of the Korean conglomerates, this is done in a more gradual manner. FIC, on the other hand, has decided that – notwithstanding successes in the developing world – building up a strong brand name for its PC and notebook systems in the near future in Europe is not yet a strategic priority. Its focus, therefore, remains on OEM production and on supplying computer assemblers with motherboards and other components. For most Taiwanese computer companies, FIC's strategy still appears to be the rule and ACER's the exception.

To what extent does the internationalization pattern of the companies as described above match the premises as put forward by the concept of late industrialization? The case studies have shown that even the strategic focus of these leading companies has, for a long time, indeed been primarily on their shopfloor operations. How then can we explain the fact that this has not prevented them from investing in Europe? In the case of Korea, we have to distinguish in this respect between the production operations in the 1980s and those in the 1990s. During the first stage of production in Europe, the companies' strengths were derived from the powerful combination of the import of cheap inputs and physical presence in the local market. Production was limited to assembly activities with minimal local content. This in fact is a hybrid mode of international business, as opposed to truly local production.

By focusing on low production costs and restricting marketing expenses to a minimum, both LGE and SEC products were positioned at the low end of the CE market. Since no direct competition took place with well known established MNCs, no additional firm-specific advantages were needed. In the 1990s, a transformation towards a more marketing orientated focus was observed for which, eventually, these early firm-specific advantages would no longer suffice. At present, it appears that their size, government (financial) support, and windfall gains (in the case of SEC) enable these companies to survive in Europe. In fact, one might argue that – although the emphasis has shifted from improvement of production processes to strengthening innovational and marketing capabilities – SEC and LGE are still in a learning process towards maturity. To be put on a par with major global competitors in these respects, substantial investments, organizational changes and a long term commitment are required. Since it may not be feasible to catch up in the near future with Japanese and European companies in terms of marketing as far as mature products (such as CTVs) are concerned, the decision that both companies have taken to concentrate on the marketing of new products (such as multimedia and electronic games) appears to be wise.

With regard to the two Taiwanese companies, it seems fair to stress that their production operations in Europe are confined to the assembly of components produced elsewhere. This, however, is characteristic for the PC and notebook industry, in which vertical integration is less common. Since the number of suppliers of computer components in Europe is limited, the nature of their production operations is not expected to change a lot in the near future. Despite the fact that ACER has recently made considerable progress in establishing its brand name in Europe, the case of FIC shows that although it is a leading company in Taiwan, even today it is still not yet in a position to shift its focus drastically away from shopfloor operations.

CONCLUSION

To what extent can these outcomes be generalized? The companies discussed here are leaders in their domestic industries. In the Taiwanese computer industry most companies focus completely on acquiring OEM contracts or developing subcontracting relationships with other, leading companies. For them, a shift beyond the first stage of strategic focus on shopfloor operations (see Figure 2) will not be feasible in the foreseeable future. This, obviously, also hampers their future internationalization. As far as the prospects of Korean firms is concerned, it appears that it is only the largest conglomerates that possess the substantial financial means and strong government support to be able to grow into fully fledged MNCs. Although smaller Korean companies have also started to invest in Europe, most of them act as component suppliers to conglomerates. The companies discussed here operate in lines of business that show a high degree of internationalization. However, more empirical research is needed to determine to what extent the prospects and limitations as outlined here also hold for companies from other industries.

NOTES

1. From now on, 'Korea' is used as shorthand for South Korea.
2. The most important early studies that were published on 'Third World' multinationals are Kumar and McLeod, 1981; Lall, 1983; Wells, 1983; and Khan, 1986.
3. As a result, wages in the industrial sector for the three years from 1988 to 1990, for instance, increased by 19.6 per cent, 25.1 per cent and 20.2 per cent in Korea. Corresponding figures for Taiwan are 10.9 per cent, 14.6 per cent and 13.5 per cent, respectively.
4. Between 1986 and 1990, for instance, the Korean Won appreciated 16.8 per cent against the US dollar. The New Taiwan dollar went up no less than 33.5 per cent against the US dollar between 1986 and 1992.
5. Of course, companies originating in early industrialized countries also focus on

improvements on the shopfloor. In that case, however, the shopfloor improvements follow the company's strategic policy (focusing on research and development and design), whereas in LIE companies the company's strategy follows these shopfloor improvements.

6. See Hikino and Amsden (1994: 308–9). According to the paradigm, the only exception relates to the case of mergers and acquisitions meant to acquire technological or marketing capabilities of other companies.

7. The Goldstar radio factory, completed in Pusan in 1959, is often seen as the start of the industry in Korea (Michell, 1988).

8. In 1994 Samsung Group's total turnover was US$ 61 billion and employment 190,000.

9. In 1989 the minimum local content requirement was raised from 20 to 40 per cent.

10. In late 1994 SEC announced a US$ 700 million investment in a fully integrated electronics and home appliance production complex in Wynyard, England.

11. Interview at headquarters with H.J. Lee, Regional Strategy Team (Europe), Global Operations Division, June 1995.

12. In Italy, for instance, a new sales organization has been established. In France, a well performing distributor has been acquired.

13. This act inaugurated the establishment of the Lucky-Goldstar Group. Lucky Chemical company had started in 1947, specializing in personal care products. In 1994 LG Group's total turnover was US$ 47.5 billion, and employment 103,000.

14. The latter first started as a JV of which LGE owned 30 per cent, but the local partner has sold out.

15. Based on data provided by the factory in Worms.

16. Interview at Central European Headquarters with W.D. Lee, April 1995.

17. Examples of the latter are monitors, motherboards, keyboards, image scanners and mice.

18. Without passing a judgement on protectionist measures taken by conventional industrialized countries, there is no doubt that the closed nature of the Korean CE market has also contributed to the hostile attitude of the EU authorities with regard to Korean products

REFERENCES

Amsden, A.H. (1989) *Asia's Next Giant: South Korea and Late Industrialization*. New York: Oxford University Press.

Amsden, A.H. (1991) 'Diffusion of Development: The Late-Industrializing Model and Greater Asia', *American Economic Review*, May, pp. 282–6.

Amsden, A.H. and Hikino, T. (1993) 'Borrowing Technology or Innovating: An Exploration of the Two Paths to Industrial Development', in R. Thomson (ed.), *Learning and Technological Change*. New York: St. Martin's Press, pp. 243–66.

Bloom, M. (1991) 'Globalisation and the Korean Electronics Industry', Conference Paper, Fontainebleau.

Bloom, M. (1992) *Technological Change in the Korean Electronics Industry*. Paris: OECD.

Dunning, J.H. (1988) *Explaining International Production*. London: Unwin Hyman.

Dunning, J.H. (1993) *Multinational Enterprises and the Global Economy*. Workingham: Addison-Wesley.

Dunning, J.H.,van Hoesel, R. and Narula, R. (1998) 'Explaining the "New" Wave of Outward FDI from Developing Countries', *International Business Review*, forthcoming.

Financial Times (1993) 8 Oct.

Financial Times (1995) 16 March.

Hikino, T. and Amsden, A.H. (1994) 'Staying Behind, Stumbling Back, Sneaking Up, Soaring Ahead: Late Industrialization in Historical Perspective', in W.J. Baumol, R.R. Nelson and E.N. Wolff (eds), *Convergence of Productivity: Cross-Country Studies and Historical Evidence*. New York, NY: Oxford University Press, pp. 285–314.

Ki, M.C. (1992) *Growth of Korean Foreign Direct Investment: Problems and Perspective*. Seoul: KIEP.

Khan, K. (ed.) (1986) *Multinationals from the South: New Actors in the International Economy*. London: Pinter Publishers.

Kumar, K. and McLeod, M.G. (eds) (1981) *Multinationals from Developing Countries*. Toronto: Lexington Books.

Lall, S. (1983) *The New Multinationals: The Spread of Third World Enterprises*. Chichester: Wiley.

McDermott, M.C. (1991) *Taiwan's Industry in World Markets – Target Europe*. The Economist

Intelligence Unit, Special Report No. 2011.

McDermott, M.C. and Young, S. (1989) *South Korea's Industry: New Directions in World Markets*. The Economist Intelligence Unit, Special Report No. 2005.

Michell, T. (1988) *From a Developing to a Newly Industrialized Country: The Republic of Korea, 1961–82*. Geneva: ILO.

Probert, J. (1991) 'Asian Direct Investment in Europe', *Euro-Asia Research Series*, Fontainebleau.

UNCTAD (1995) *World Investment Report 1995*. Geneva: UN.

van Hoesel, R. (1992) 'Multinational Enterprises from Developing Countries with Investments in Developed Economies: Some Theoretical Considerations', *CIMDA Discussion Papers*, 1992/E/6, Antwerp.

van Hoesel, R. (1996) 'Taiwan: Foreign Direct Investment and the Transformation of the Economy', in J.H. Dunning and R. Narula (eds), *Foreign Direct Investment, Governments and Economic Restructuring: Catalysts of Change*. London: Routledge, pp. 280–315.

Wells, L.T., Jr (1983) *Third World Multinationals: The Rise of Foreign Investment from Developing Countries*. Cambridge, MA: MIT Press.

Conclusion: Korean Business and Management – The End of the Model?

CHRIS ROWLEY and JOHNGSEOK BAE

The Korean[1] economy has grown rapidly, earning plaudits. Between 1970 and 1997, Korean gross domestic product (GDP) grew at an annual average of 8.4 per cent (*The Economist*, 1998b). However, the recent financial crisis has raised questions about the underpinnings and longevity of economic success in Asia, and has reminded us to be sceptical of pundits and eponymous populist predictions concerning the region. The 'miracle' may be a sham, built on governments pouring cheap credit into favoured firms and cosy relationships insulating businesses from market forces and encouraging excessive borrowing and wasteful use of resources. Several perspectives can guide the analysis and evaluation of industrialization, from 'state' versus 'market', 'internal' versus 'external', and 'macro' versus 'micro'. Companies in Korea as 'latecomers' have pursued 'catch-up' strategies. Yet, Korean corporate capabilities still reside in a *restricted* number of industries, firms and functions (production), and are poor elsewhere, such as in marketing, technology (design and development) and organization, and dynamic and innovative small and medium-sized enterprises (SMEs). Many factors regarded once as sources of Korea's success are now seen as weaknesses. The future challenges facing Korea include its *dirigiste* economy, organizational structures and governance, financial transparency and labour market flexibility. While there are undoubted problems, its urgent need for reform is not insurmountable.

We will re-examine some of the key points and perspectives of the earlier contributions before detailing the key problems faced by the Korean model of business and management in the wake of the recent financial contagion in Asia and its Korean strain. We then note some of the reforms attempted early on in the crisis to cure the problems with this 'Asian Tiger' in the areas of business and labour. In this, the government remains a key component and prescriber of remedies.

SOME LESSONS LEARNED?

What can we learn from the contributions in this volume? First, there are several perspectives, each with merits, from which we can analyse and evaluate the process of industrialization (state versus free market; internal

Chris Rowley, City University Business School, London; Johngseok Bae, Hanyang University, Korea.

versus external; and macro versus micro). When the market proved inadequate, the government facilitated the 'learning processes' of firms. When industrial activities became more complex and dynamic, business took the initiatives. An interesting point is that among the three industrial actors of employers, employees and state, the state played a crucial first role in the early stage of the industrialization process of Korea; then management, especially the *chaebols*; the next cause of change may be innovative individuals. We need a panoramic viewpoint. It is safe to say that Korean industrialization and economic growth were attributable to the facilitating role of the government, well educated and hard working people, the entrepreneurship of Korean management, and specific historical and geographical conditions (see also Cathie[2] in this volume).

Second, many factors once regarded as a source of Korean economic success are now actually seen as among the sources of more current failure. Some of the very factors that brought rapid economic development and industrialization are now construed as obstacles to future advancement. For instance, government intervention, the *chaebols* and their structure, militaristic organization, and the nationalistic homogeneity in culture and language (limiting inward investment and more 'professional' management, such as in personnel practices), were all once seen as significant assets, but are now presented as serious liabilities and generating social costs.

Third, the 'late industrialization' paradigm shows different characteristics from those of the 'early industrialization' model. Leading firms in 'firstcomer' countries gained competitive advantages[3] through inventions or innovations, resulting from research and development (R&D). In firstcomer firms, production may become less important as time goes by because firms strategically pursue the international distribution of operations mainly through original equipment manufacture (van Hoesel). This is related to theories concerning the location of production. As we noted earlier, a wealth of early literature exists in this area (Vernon, 1966; Hirsch, 1967), though it has been moderated (Vernon, 1979; Utterback, 1994) and criticized (Rowley, 1992, 1998a). However, latecomer firms pursue catch-up strategies through imitating (borrowing or learning). According to the theories of technology transfer, catching-up countries acquire 'mature' (rather than 'fluid' or 'transition') technologies,[4] focusing first on engineering and production efforts (Kim, 1997; see Rowley, 1992, for an overview of work on technology cycles). These groups of theories imply that catch up firms would build production capability first and then others.

Finally, related to the above, Korean corporate capabilities have been in a *restricted* number of industries (mainly electronics, and especially semiconductors), in a *limited* number of firms (largely in the few biggest *chaebols*), and with a *constrained* source of competitive advantage (with weaknesses in non-production capabilities such as marketing, technological and overall organizational skills). Other industries, except ones such as electronics and automobiles, are still in the catch-up stage. Yet, even in electronics, while leadership appeared in some sectors (such as the memory area), others (like the non-memory sphere) fell behind. In addition, only the large conglomerates had enough human, financial and physical resources to become truly global players. In contrast, SMEs have shown little competitiveness, one result of which is the *chaebols'* high dependency upon foreign suppliers (see Castley). Some recent government support has been promised to encourage SMEs, and for them to manufacture and supply more high technology and high valued parts (Chung *et al.*, 1997). However, SMEs are often naively presented as dynamic creators of jobs and innovation. This generalization can certainly be challenged, as many SMEs remain little more than more traditional-type 'sweatshops', with very little innovation (or employment) creation.

CHALLENGES AND FUTURE TASKS

Korea was the eleventh largest economy in the world, previously celebrated as the most robust and healthy of the 'Asian Tigers', whose largest *chaebols* included household names, and which invested and built plants around the world. Yet, this rapid growth rate actually helped conceal weaknesses and led to complacency and slowness to act at signs of trouble, or even to admit policies were flawed (*The Economist*, 1998b). Its *dirigiste* economy, including bureaucrats allocating capital and 'picking winners', has been hit by the Asian contagion. The big engines of Korean economic growth, the *chaebols*, are misfiring and now stalling. There are early reports of cutbacks on Korean corporate overseas investments: LG's £1.7 billion (Europe's largest inward investment) TV and microchip plant in Wales has been delayed, Hyundai's £850 million semiconductor plant in Scotland has been postponed, and Samsung's £425 million microchip plant in North East England has been deferred (Parsley and Lorenz, 1998). Large scale job losses, with unemployment to rising to over one million by late 1998, are predicted. For Koreans, there has been the humiliating image of Korea going 'cap in hand' for a US$ 55 billion IMF bailout (Burton, 1997).

There are extra problems in that many Asian economies have simultaneously hit problems, and given that a large proportion of trade (two-thirds of exports) is with each other, difficulties will be magnified (*The Economist*, 1998b). Other problems stem from social changes and an aging population in an era of eroding family ties and cohesiveness, requiring massive spending and taxation to fund health systems, education (ibid.) and Korea's 'pay as you go' pension scheme (Heller, 1997). A further big fear is the possible collapse of North Korea and the huge economic costs of potential reunification. This is indicated in the following comparisons. In 1996, while North Korea's gross national product (GNP) was US$ 22 billion, South Korea's was US$ 450 billion, with GNP per capita of just US$ 857 in the North, but over US$ 10,000 in the South (Chung *et al.*, 1997).

Given this, what are the future tasks that Korean firms need to undertake? They face severe challenges both domestically and internationally (see also Chung *et al.*, 1997). The areas awaiting repair include obtaining US dollars; that is, restoring creditworthiness in the eyes of international investors, while a better export performance due to a devalued Won will necessarily earn them dollars – the Won fell by 50 per cent at the end of 1997 (Cathie). Other areas include enhancing financial transparency, changing governance systems, consolidating firms, and motivating employees alienated and distressed by harsh work regimes (see Lindauer *et al.*, 1997; Lee and Lindauer, 1997) and more recent layoffs and threats of future redundancies. These conditions provide *chaebols* with several dilemmas. These include how to: (1) gain competitive advantage with fearful employees; (2) invest more in research and development (R&D) in financially stringent times; and (3) simultaneously pursue strategies for both catching up and sustaining existing competitive advantages.

Numerical Flexibility in a Cold Climate

The first dilemma is related to the issue of labour market flexibility, especially in its numerical dimension. In January 1998 a Tripartite Committee was formed to discuss several crisis related issues, of which the legalization of layoffs was the most contentious. We have already observed that an earlier attempt to introduce such labour market numerical flexibility resulted in conflict (Bae *et al.*, 1997). Neither is labour unrest (and social dissatisfaction) 'new' to Korea (see Lindauer *et al.*, 1997). The Committee was made up of representatives from two major labour groups (the Federation of Korean Trade Unions or FKTU, and the Korean Confederation of Trade Unions or KCTU), business and the government. The two labour group leaders persistently demanded full supplementary measures and *chaebol* reforms *before* legalizing mass layoffs. In contrast, Korean firms sought labour market flexibility and downsizing *at the same time*, difficult tasks to successfully undertake together (Leipziger, 1988).

Furthermore, 'rigidities' need not necessarily be taken as the polar opposites to 'flexibilities' (Dore, 1986) or as mutually exclusive – the former can actually enhance the latter. For example, some structures perceived as rigidities or 'inflexibilities' (such a 'safety net' of labour provision) can increase the likelihood of numerical flexibility (by reducing workers' fears). Also, enhanced numerical flexibility (that is, easier 'hire and fire') may reduce pressures on firms to compete by other means, including by upgrading (and the requisite investment in skills) and thus undermine longer term competitiveness. In contrast, rigidities may force firms to attempt this, to climb the technological ladder to make more advanced goods via investment in the latest capital equipment and functional flexibility utilizing skilled employees. Thus, rigidity can aid flexibility. Nevertheless, it seems that the Korean version of the Chinese 'iron rice bowl' or 'jobs for life' approach has been corroded (see also contributions to Rowley, 1998b) and may continue to weaken.

Extra difficulties with the Korean labour market situation include the following. Working life is reported as harsh, unsafe, with low satisfaction and long working weeks (Lee and Lindauer, 1997). Also, as Park Fun-koo, President of the Korean Labour Institute put it, 'Losing your job means going on the street. If management aggressively pushes mass redundancies, they will encounter resistance from workers' (quoted in Burton, 1998b: 9). Neither will a reinvigorated economy necessarily reduce worker discontent – its roots in the past lay in the lack of political freedoms (and uneven distribution of wealth (Lindauer et al., 1997). However, some of these sorts of problem may be ameliorated somewhat with the recent path-breaking legislation (see Table 1).

TABLE 1
RECENT REFORMS WITH LABOUR RELATIONS IMPLICATIONS

* Improved social benefits
* Increased unemployment funds (from Won 1,600 billion to Won 2,800 billion)
* Eased eligibility rules for unemployment funds
* New union rights to organize (e.g. for teachers)
* State employees banned from forming unions can organize 'consultative' groups
* Unions allowed to engage in political activity

Source: compiled from Burton, 1998a.

Nevertheless, a further reason why mass layoffs or downsizing programmes often fail is that 'employees who survive the purges become narrow-minded, self-absorbed, and risk-averse' (Noe et al., 1997: 274), which eventually brings negative effects to organizational learning and innovation. There is also the problem of the so-called 'survivors syndrome': employees who were not made redundant simply wait fearfully for the next retrenchment round and possibly their 'turn'. Indeed, fear of unemployment seems to be increasing in Korea. A survey of 1,500 people working at nationwide companies with five or more employees, recently conducted by the Korea Labour Institute, indicated that about 40 per cent feared losing their jobs. This may be exacerbated by the spread of redundancies from blue collar and manual jobs to include more non-manual and managerial positions, creating an epidemic, as it seemingly has elsewhere, of 'white-collar blues' (Heckscher, 1995). Such trends run counter to the scenario, now so often predicted, of future competition underpinned by 'quality', 'service' and 'committed' and 'resourceful' human resources (see Hochschild, 1983).

The Chaebols: Reforms, Restructuring and Retrenchment versus Increasing Investments

The second dilemma concerns the organization of enterprises and management and state involvement. It is believed that Korea 'has been East Asia's most controlled and distorted economy, dominated by the bloated *chaebols*' (*The Economist*, 1998b: 15). Although the *chaebols* have shown strong production capability, we have seen that elsewhere they still lag behind. Globalization of the economy also requires Korean firms to enhance international management capability (for example, coordination ability and inter-subsidiary networks). The *chaebols* should actually invest more, such as in R&D, and increase 'minimum efficiency scales' and quality – but now during more financially frugal times. Yet, many firms have recently reduced their investments in new projects and R&D. Also, high investment for investments' sake is not always either successful or a sign of strength. It has been estimated that as of 1997 the *chaebols* had bad debts of twice GDP – some US$ 500 billion, or more than four times equity (Burton, 1997). Business will also be affected by recent financial restructuring plans, as Table 2 outlines. Furthermore, 'traditional' Korean management style is portrayed as authoritarian, with what has been labelled 'relation-oriented' personnel management based on family, school and regional ties (Chung *et al.*, 1997). There have been some attempts to reform some of this, such as Samsung's attempts to change such management culture: job applicants are no longer required to identify the schools they attended, and the group secretariat is banned from meddling in the personnel affairs of its subsidiaries (ibid.).

TABLE 2
RECENT FINANCIAL RESTRUCTURING PLANS AND IMPLICATIONS

* Independence to central bank – reduces the overwhelming influence of finance ministry
* Opening debt and equity markets to foreign investors – stimulates competition and promotes emphasis on credit analysis
* Closure/merger of financial institutions – liquidates bad loans and curbs borrowing
* Reduce *chaebol* bank lending – forces use of capital markets for funds, and subject to greater discipline of investors and shareholders
* Production of consolidated financial accounts – promotes corporate transparency
* Limits on mutual/cross debt guarantees among *chaebol* subsidiaries – unravels groups and forces them to focus on 'core' business and competencies
* Fewer state bail-outs via subsidies and tax breaks
* Reform bankruptcy procedures – encourages accelerated liquidation of failed businesses

Source: compiled from Burton, 1997, 1998a.

On the restructuring of the *chaebols*, then President-elect Kim Dae-jung and his advisers initially undertook an aggressive reform drive. At a meeting with four *chaebol* leaders in January 1998 it was agreed to reform business practices in line with international standards. Specifically, it was pledged that companies would adopt a consolidated financial statement system and cease the practice of inter-subsidiary loan guarantees as early as possible with a view to enhancing managerial transparency. The old practice of cross-loan guarantees had helped the *chaebols* gain easy access to bank loans, so fuelling reckless expansion (and increasing the costs of loans for SMEs). At the same time, this practice has exposed the *chaebols* to potentially catastrophic chain bankruptcies involving their subsidiaries. However, the presidential economic emergency committee recently decided not to force the *chaebols* to conduct 'big deals' (such as swapping companies among themselves), after discontent was expressed with the approach of this economic team. The reason that 'swaps' were required was that it is regarded as a process of reform that would enhance corporate competitiveness by encouraging several core firms per *chaebol*, rather than each having so many diverse subsidiaries. At this time, it is hard to say how successful the reforms will be.

Routes to Competition: Caught between Two Stools?

Even with successful changes on both management and labour sides, a dilemma remains for Korea. Somewhat simplistically, we can perceive two types of competition: the use of cheap and poorly skilled workers for low value products versus the use of expensive but high skilled workers for expensive, value added, quality production (see Rowley and Lewis, 1996). This issue is linked to the idea of a 'sandwich economy' (see also Deyo, 1996). Korean firms have been challenged on the one hand by low-price developing countries, and on the other by quality based economically advanced countries. Against the first competitor group, Korean firms need to have a strategy to sustain competitive advantage; and, at the same time, against the second competitor group they need to have a catch-up strategy. The use of mid-technologies by the leading firms of latecomers can also be regarded as their strategy because shopfloor improvement is the source of their comparative advantage (van Hoesel).

Indicative of this is a comparison of monthly manufacturing pay (in sterling terms) in a recent survey (Fleming, 1998). One the one hand, Korea (£522) compares very well with Japan £1,953), the US (£2,194) and Germany (£3,723). Yet, on the other hand, it seems impossible for Korea to compete on this dimension with other Asian economies: Malaysia (£170), Thailand (£63), and especially China (£39) and now Indonesia (£13). Obviously, there are reliability, methodological and comparative problems with work of this nature and its use, including currency movements, what 'pay' includes, as in terms of social costs paid by employers, cost of living, and so on. Also, much depends on productivity differences: we cannot simply compare labour costs on their own (detailed analysis of this sort is beyond this present piece). This situation is made even more difficult with competitive currency devaluations. For example, in 1996 Thailand's monthly pay rate had been £126 and Indonesia's £48 (ibid.). The problems (and requisite changes needed) in 'beggar thy neighbour' policies and their contributions to national competitiveness are discussed in Boltho (1996).

Critically, as Kim shows, it is almost impossible for Korean firms' to gain competitive advantage through low prices maintained with low labour costs. Competitive advantage from other sources (quality, speed, innovation, types of production, and so on) is a more realistic avenue over the longer term. So, management and firms need to 'choose' (or be 'guided' towards) the second route to competition. This can be achieved by such factors as employee competencies and commitment. These factors can be enhanced through long term attachments and extensive training and empowerment (Pfeffer, 1994; Bae *et al.*, 1997). However, in practice, there exists an inherent dilemma: how to obtain such competitive advantage with 'anxious' employees (see Pfeffer, 1994; Levine, 1995). Korean firms may need to pay attention to Geus's (1997: 202) suggestion that: 'If corporate health falters, the priority should be on mobilizing the maximum human potential, on restoring or maintaining trust and civic behavior, and on increasing professionalism and good citizenship'. A cost minimizing approach can in the short term 'solve' issues such as productivity, but then may simply prepare the ground for another pitfall in the long run (Nolan and O'Donnell, 1995). This can be by preventing the creation, enhancement and acknowledgement of the competencies and commitments of human assets.

This sort of pincer movement poses threats to Korean firms; however, they are also opportunities with potential benefits if the upgrading route is followed. The future positioning of Korean firms among other groups of competitors (firstcomer firms, other latecomer firms such as the Taiwanese, and 'late-latecomers' such as the Chinese) will be highly dependent upon success in their 'second learning process'.

From 'Hype' to 'Hope'?

At one extreme, recent events in Asia may lead us to view much previous work in the area as little more than sophistry, an illusion conjured out of thin air, and to see the Korean model as not really a miracle but more a mirage. An interesting exercise is to re-read those numerous pundits who 'got it wrong' with regard to the Asian 'miracle' (see *The Economist*, 1998a). For instance, in historical perspective, Asian economic performance was neither never really 'miraculous', given that Asia contains 60 per cent of the world's population, nor 'new', as the area was producing 33 per cent GNP back in 1900 (ibid.). Is such scepticism especially applicable to the Korean model? Much of Korean business does lie moribund, weakened, and some even mortally damaged, and technologically dynamic SMEs remain nascent and underdeveloped. Labour remains anxious and apprehensive, facing threats of redundancies and unemployment.

Yet, we should not forget undoubted Korean successes – there may well be something to salvage from the wreckage of the Korean model. In February 1998 the Korean Parliament approved landmark twin track legislation on corporate and labour reforms (as discussed earlier) to promote industrial restructuring and encourage foreign investors in a nation that had previously shunned them (Burton, 1998a). There needs to be a balance struck between, on the one hand corporate changes to enhance capabilities and upgrading, and on the other support and protections to enhance labour market flexibility of the 'right' sort. Given this, and other changes, Icarus may well learn to fly again. Then once more the Korean economy will produce something that, while not on the 'miracle' scale, will none the less still be impressive.

ACKNOWLEDGEMENTS

Our thanks to Robert Fitzgerald for his perceptive lexical points and to Outi Aarnio for enhancing our economic clarity. The normal disclaimers apply.

NOTES

1. From now on, 'Korea' is used as shorthand for South Korea.
2. In this contribution, unreferenced authors refer to their contributions in this volume.
3. However, see again the important note 3 in our Introduction concerning key caveats on the concept of 'competitiveness', especially Krugman, 1994, 1996.
4. The stages of technological trajectory (fluid, transitions, specific) are from the influential and famous work by Abernathy and Utterback (1978). See also Utterback and Abernathy, 1975; Abernathy, 1978; and developments such as Abernathy *et al.*, 1983; Abernathy and Clark, 1985; and more recently Utterback, 1994.

REFERENCES

Abernathy, W.J. (1978) *The Productivity Dilemma: Roadblock to Innovation in the Automobile Industry*. Baltimore, MD: Johns Hopkins University Press.

Abernathy, W.J. and Utterback, J.M. (1978) 'Patterns of Industrial Innovation', *Technology Review*, Vol. 80, No. 7, pp. 41–8.

Abernathy, W.J., Clark, K.B. and Kantow, A.M. (1983) *Industrial Renaissance: Producing a Competitive Future for America*. New York, NY: Basic Books.

Abernathy, W.J. and Clark, K.B. (1985) 'Innovation: Mapping the Winds of Creative Destruction', *Research Policy*, Vol. 14, No. 1, pp. 3–22.

Bae, J., Rowley, C., Kim, Dong-heon and Lawler, J. (1997) 'Korean Industrial Relations at the Crossroads: The Recent Labour Troubles', *Asia Pacific Business Review*, Vol. 3, No. 3, pp. 148–60.

Boltho, A. (1996) 'The Assessment: International Competitiveness', *Oxford Review of Economic Policy*, Vol. 1, No. 3, pp. 1–16.

Burton, J. (1997) 'Painful Prospect', *Financial Times*, 8 Dec., p. 8.

Burton, J. (1998a) 'S. Korean Reforms To Boost Restructuring', *Financial Times*, 16 Feb., p. 4.

Burton, J. (1998b) 'The Good Dae-Jung', *Financial Times*, 28 Feb., p. 9.

Chung, K.H., Lee, H.C. and Jung, K.H. (1997) *Korean Management: Global Strategy and Cultural Transformation*. Berlin: de Gruyter.

Deyo, F.C. (1996) (ed.) *Social Reconstructions of the World Automobile Industry: Competition, Power and Industrial Flexibility*. London: Macmillan.

Dore, R. (1986) *Flexible Rigidities: Industrial Policy and Structural Adjustment in the Japanese Economy, 1970–1980*. London: Athlone.

Economist, The (1998a) 'Re-Reviewing the Pundits', 28 Feb., pp. 109–10.

Economist, The (1998b) 'East Asian Economic Survey: Frozen Miracle', 7 March, pp. 1–20.

Fleming, R. (1998) reported in 'Wave of Asian Exports Set to Batter UK Firms', *Daily Mail*, 5 March, p. 6.

Geus, Aris de (1997) *The Living Company*. Boston, MA: Harvard Business School Press.

Heckscher, C. (1995) *White-Collar Blues: Management Loyalties in an Age of Corporate Restructuring*. New York, NY: Basic Books.

Heller, P. (1997) *Again in the Asian Tigers: Challenges for Fiscal Policy*. IMF Working Paper, Oct.

Hirsch, S. (1967) *Location of Industry and International Competitiveness*. Oxford: Clarendon.

Hochschild, A. (1983) *The Managed Heart: Commercialization of Human Feeling*. California: California University Press.

Kim, L. (1997) *Imitation to Innovation: The Dynamics of Korea's Technological Learning*. Boston, MA: Harvard Business School Press.

Krugman, P.R. (1994) 'Competitveness: A Dangerous Obsession', *Foreign Affairs*, Vol. 73, No. 2, pp. 28–44.

Krugman, P.R. (1996) 'Making Sense of the Competitiveness Debate', *Oxford Review of Economic Policy*, Vol. 12, No. 3, pp. 17–25.

Lee, J.-L. and Lindauer, D.L. (1997) 'The Quality of Working Life', in D.L. Lindauer, J.-G. Kim, J.-W. Lee, H.-S. Lim, J.-Y. Son and E. Vogel, *The Strains of Economic Growth: Labor Unrest and Social Dissatisfaction in Korea*. Cambridge, MA: Harvard Institute for International Development, pp. 77–92.

Leipziger, D.M. (1988) 'Industrial Restructuring in Korea', *World Development*, Vol. 16, No. 1, pp. 121–35.

Levine, D.I. (1995) *Reinventing the Workplace: How Business and Employees Can Both Win*.

Washington, DC: The Brookings Institution.

Lindauer, D.L, Kim, J.-G., Lee, J.-W., Lim, H.-S., Son, J-Y. and Vogel, E. (1997) *The Strains of Economic Growth: Labor Unrest and Social Dissatisfaction in Korea*. Cambridge, MA: Harvard Institute for International Development.

Noe, R.A., Hollenbeck, J.R., Gerhart, B. and Wright, P.M. (1997) *Human Resource Management: Gaining a Competitive Advantage*, 2nd edn. Chicago, IL: Irwin.

Nolan, P. and O'Donnell, K. (1995) 'Industrial Relations and Productivity', in P.K. Edwards (ed.), *Industrial Relations: Theory and Practice in Britain*. Oxford: Blackwell, pp. 397–433.

Parsley, D. and Lorenz, A. (1998) 'Taiwan to Invest £1bn in UK', *The Sunday Times*, 15 March, p. 3:1.

Pfeffer, J. (1994) *Competitive Advantage through People: Unleashing the Power of the Workforce*. Boston, MA: Harvard Business School Press.

Rowley, C. (1992) 'Technological Change in a Mature Industry: The Case of Ceramics', Unpublished D.Phil. Thesis, Nuffield College, University of Oxford.

Rowley, C. (1998a) 'Manufacturing Mobility? Internationalization, Change and Continuity', *Journal of General Management*, Vol. 23, No. 3, pp. 21–34.

Rowley, C. (ed.) (1998b) *HRM in the Asia Pacific Region: Convergence Questioned*. London and Portland, OR: Cass.

Rowley, C. and Lewis, M. (1996) 'Greater China at the Crossroads? Convergence, Culture and Competitiveness', *Asia Pacific Business Review*, Vol. 2, No. 3, pp. 1–22.

Utterback, J.M. (1994) *Mastering the Dynamics of Innovation: How Companies can Seize Opportunities in the Face of Technological Change*. Cambridge, MA: Harvard University Press.

Utterback, J.M. and Abernathy, W.J. (1975) 'A Dynamic Model of Product and Process Innovation', *Omega*, Vol. 3, No. 6, pp. 639–56.

Vernon, R. (1966) 'International Investment and International Trade in the Product Cycle', *Quarterly Journal of Economics*, Vol. 80, pp. 190–207.

Vernon, R. (1979) 'The Product Life Cycle Hypothesis in a New Industrial Environment', *Bulletin of Economics and Statistics*, Vol. 41, pp. 265–7.

Abstracts

Introduction: The Icarus Paradox in Korean Business and Management *by Chris Rowley and Johngseok Bae*

Some writers argue that modern history reveals that countries pass through 'cycles' in economic leadership. The 'forerunners' of industrialization used inventions and innovations as the major sources of their growth. On the other hand, newly industrializing countries, labelled 'latecomers' *vis-à-vis* the first groups, relied more on imitating, borrowing, or learning advanced technological and organizational capabilities to achieve national industrialization and eventually to gain national competitiveness. For some time, many have viewed such economies, especially the 'Asian Tigers', as a major force that will lead future world economic growth. However, such expectations have diminished with the recent financial crisis and contagion in Asia. The subject matter covered here includes the sources of economic growth and industrialization, the 'catch-up' strategies of firms, and foreign investment. The causes of the recent financial crisis, and future possibilities for the Korean model of business and management, are also analysed.

Financial Contagion in East Asia and the Origins of the Economic and Financial Crisis in Korea, *by John Cathie*

In this article the major elements of the 30 year old Asian development model are examined in the light of the financial crisis in the region. The notion of a common model is examined and found to be overstated. The monetary crisis in Asia has affected countries to different degrees, with Indonesia and Korea being particularly weakened. Korea has two major economic problems which can be traced to economic policies established in the 1960s. First, the industrial organization of the economy under a few industrial conglomerates, which has outlived its usefulness and is now a major source of the troubles in the economy. The conglomerates have been responsible for an investment policy where risk has been pushed to recklessness and the rate of return on capital employed is meagre. Second, banking policy, which is best characterized as a severe form of 'moral hazard'. Both of these policies, while having played major parts in past economic successes, are now the main cause of a weakened economy in a globalized world.

The Korean Electronics Industry: The Japanese Role in its Growth, *by Robert J. Castley*

Korea's electronics industry has developed to the point where it accounts for an increasing share of output, exports and employment. Its spectacular growth can be largely attributed to its rapid expansion to become the dominant export, accounting for more than a quarter of the total. To determine the causes of this performance, this contribution will look at both 'internal' (government policy regimes, incentives) and 'external' factors. It argues that domestic policies were only effective in so far as they were supported by external factors. Such export-orientated industrialization includes a cycle between investment, imports competitiveness and exports.

Latecomer Catch-up Strategies in Electronics: Samsung of Korea and ACER of Taiwan, *by Mike Hobday*

Very little is known about the strategies by which East Asian firms acquired foreign technology and managed to 'catch up' in electronics. Unlike Western and Japanese innovation 'leaders' and 'followers', East Asian firms are 'latecomers', dislocated from advanced markets, demanding buyers and international sources of technology. This work examines the cases of two leading latecomers – Samsung Electronics of Korea and ACER of Taiwan – to generate insights into how electronics manufacturers overcame barriers to entry and became strong competitors on the world stage. The aim is to highlight the sources, paths and mechanisms of learning in the two firms, relating these patterns to corporate strategy, organization and performance. This contribution argues that latecomers reversed the traditional research and development centred pattern of innovation, travelling backwards along the product life cycle, from mature to early stages. A simple model is put forward to show how latecomer firms progressed up the technological ladder within the electronics subcontract system called original equipment manufacture. Attention is also drawn to theoretical implications and the strengths, remaining weaknesses and future challenges facing latecomer firms.

Global Competition and Latecomer Production Strategies: Samsung of Korea in China, *by Youngsoo Kim*

This contribution illustrates how latecomer multinational companies (MNCs) have organized international production activities and maintained their competitive advantage under growing global competition. In doing so, an interdisciplinary approach, including an evolutionary theory of MNCs, global strategic management, and organizational and technological learning, is adopted through the case study of Samsung Electronics as a sample latecomer MNC. Samsung reveals that competition in the electronics industry in China is based on the differential capabilities of players in the market, and their ability to transfer and improve these capabilities faster than competitors. Latecomer MNCs' foreign subsidiaries are under strong pressure to be actively involved in design and product development activities near to production facilities. In order to gain a sustainable competitive advantage, foreign subsidiaries of latecomer MNCs need to rapidly improve their product innovation capability by combining knowledge transferred from the MNC headquarters and global subsidiaries' networks with information about consumer requirements in the foreign location.

The Emergence of Korean and Taiwanese Multinationals in Europe: Prospects and Limitations, *by Roger van Hoesel*

Although the outward orientation of the Korean and Taiwanese economies in the past was confined to their export activities, during the last decade and a half they have emerged as important home countries of overseas investment. In this contribution, special attention is paid to their investment activities in Europe, about which very little is known. After a short theoretical discussion of their 'deviant' ('late') industrialization patterns, the investments of two Korean (consumer electronics) and two Taiwanese (computer) companies in Europe are examined in detail. Special attention is paid to their actual operations in the region, the motivations to invest and the problems faced in building up a strong position in this part of the industrialized world. It will be shown that the late industrialization nature of the Korean and Taiwanese economies has considerably influenced their internationalization patterns.

Conclusion: Korean Business and Management – the End of the Model? *by Chris Rowley and Johngseok Bae*

Recent financial crisis has raised questions about the underpinnings and longevity of economic success in Asia, and has reminded us to be sceptical of pundits and the eponymous populist predictions relating to the region. Several perspectives can guide the analysis and evaluation of industrialization, from 'state' versus 'market', 'internal' versus 'external', and 'macro' versus 'micro'. Companies in Korea as 'latecomers' have pursued 'catch-up' strategies. However, Korean corporate capabilities reside in a *restricted* number of industries, firms and functions (production), and are poor elsewhere, such as in marketing, technology (design and development) and organization, and small and medium-sized enterprises. Furthermore, many factors regarded once as sources of Korea's success are now seen as weaknesses. The future challenges facing Korea include its *dirigiste* economy, organizational structures and governance, financial transparency and labour market flexibility. While there are undoubted problems, its urgent tasks are not insurmountable.

Index